FACE TIME

FACE TIME

Event Planning for Business Success

ASIF ZAIDI

A COMPLETE GUIDE FOR DESIGNING, PLANNING, MARKETING, AND STAGING AN EVENT

BOCA RATON PUBLIC LIBRARY
BOCA RATON, FLORIDA

FACE TIME
EVENT PLANNING FOR BUSINESS SUCCESS

Copyright © 2018 Asif Zaidi.

All rights reserved. No part of this book may be used or reproduced by any means, graphic, electronic, or mechanical, including photocopying, recording, taping or by any information storage retrieval system without the written permission of the author except in the case of brief quotations embodied in critical articles and reviews.

iUniverse books may be ordered through booksellers or by contacting:

iUniverse
1663 Liberty Drive
Bloomington, IN 47403
www.iuniverse.com
1-800-Authors (1-800-288-4677)

Because of the dynamic nature of the Internet, any web addresses or links contained in this book may have changed since publication and may no longer be valid. The views expressed in this work are solely those of the author and do not necessarily reflect the views of the publisher, and the publisher hereby disclaims any responsibility for them.

Any people depicted in stock imagery provided by Getty Images are models, and such images are being used for illustrative purposes only. Certain stock imagery © Getty Images.

ISBN: 978-1-5320-4787-9 (sc)
ISBN: 978-1-5320-4786-2 (e)

Library of Congress Control Number: 2018905134

Print information available on the last page.

iUniverse rev. date: 05/21/2018

CONTENTS

Preface vii

1. Basics 1
- How to Plan a Business Event 3
- Types of Business Events 6
- Proactive Planning 11
- Planning for Success 14

2. Strategy 17
- Business Event Strategy 19
- Shaping Your Story 24
- Exhibiting Thought Leadership 28

3. Target Market 33
- Determining Your Target Audience 35
- Shaping the Event for Your Audience 38

4. The Venue 41
- Location, Location, Location 43
- How to Select a Venue 46
- Setting Up a Venue 52
- Using Tents 55

5. Marketing 57
- All About Publicity 59
- Building Your Image 63

- Marketing Your Message 66
- Sales Tools 69
- Giveaways and Promo Material 71
- Lead Generation 74

6. The Team 77
- Your Event Team 79
- External Event Partners 84
- Your Team on the Day 88

7. Organization 95
- All About Timing 97
- Minding the Details 102
- Preparing and Monitoring the Budget 105
- Contingency Planning 111
- Safety 117
- Transportation 124

8. Food and Drink 127
- Party Fare 129
- Business Meals 132
- Cocktails 135

9. Guests 139
- Designing the Guest Experience 141
- Minding Your Guests 148
- Receiving Your Guests 151

10. Productivity 155
- How to Measure Success 157
- After the Event 162
- How to Measure Productivity 165

Appendix: Checklist for Event Materials and Logistics 169

PREFACE

Organizing events—whether you own your business or work for a company—is an essential part of doing business. Events open doors for sales opportunities and offer great networking. Events also deepen relationships with customers, partners, employees, media, and the market. As someone who is passionate about creating memorable events within reasonable budgets, I believe that the expertise I have gathered from 20 years of organizing events, across a number of countries, will be of significant use to you.

Organizing an effective event requires the same skills and requisites regardless of your job title. However, it is a team job and you have to understand that everyone in your company or business has to play a role. It is essential to garner support and coordination at all levels.

The insight and knowledge in this book covers any event, regardless of its purpose and type, whether it is held at a club, a convention center, a hotel, a park, or at home. This book will not only show you how to organize various types of events but it also goes well beyond logistics and planning to explain how you can leverage an event to maximum effect. It explains how sales and marketing can best coordinate to make sure that all strategic events are integrated with the overall marketing plans of the business. It also shows you how to set, pursue, and achieve strategic goals by accentuating customer experience throughout the event cycle and extracting value from every interaction.

1. BASICS

HOW TO PLAN A BUSINESS EVENT

"Plans are nothing. Planning is everything."
Albert Einstein

Whether you are planning a corporate party, a product launch, a customer reception, or any other event, careful planning is an essential prerequisite for success. You have to plan your event in fine detail, but must also have a plan B for probable contingencies. Organizing an event, however, is not rocket science; it takes only common sense and attention to detail. Let's look at some major aspects of event planning.

Define Your Purpose

Keep in mind the primary objective of your event. That is, why are you holding it in the first place? Make sure that the objective justifies its cost. How you plan and organize your event is a function of your budget and your event's objective. For example, if the objective is to capture media attention, then money spent on attracting journalists to your event is an important element in your budget. Such an event must ensure ample photo opportunities and high-quality interviews.

Make a Budget

First up, the financial commitment to the event must be calibrated. You need to decide on how much you want to spend so that you can plan accordingly. Whether you need approvals or not, start with a rough estimate of costs. That will also help you see how you are choosing to spend your money. Make a detailed wish list, and then select the essential items. The rest of the items on the list are optional; they can be factored in once you have allocated costs to the essential items. Your preliminary cost estimates should also allow a 10%–20% cushion for cost overruns and unforeseen expenses.

Start Early Planning

Once you have defined the purpose and allocated the necessary funds, you are ready to make an initial plan. The main things to consider at this stage include deciding whether you need outside professional help, setting up an internal event team, establishing the type of event to have, and determining suitable timing. Look at your target audience to determine the type of event that will suit them the best. Bringing in professional help early on can actually save you money. If you need help with inviting the right people and getting press coverage, consider hiring a good public relations company. If you need help with the conception and the organization of the event, engage a creative director.

While setting up your internal event team, make sure that you match the right skills with the tasks involved. In order to avoid confusion and adhere to the budget, have one person deal with suppliers.

Make a detailed timeline of all tasks involved and meticulously follow its progress.

Visualize Your Event

Imagining the entire sequence of your event can help you address any potential problems in the planning stages. It will also help you decide the staffing you will need to greet and entertain your guests in the manner you envisage.

Ponder the ambience you want to create, the tempo, the flow, the content, and the program of proceedings from beginning to end. List every element that you want to include, and then decide on the must-haves to make your event a success. That will allow you to plan and budget in the order of priority.

Build Your Image

Remember that your event is the image of your organization to the outside world and your own image within the organization. It can work both for and against you.

Think beforehand what perception of your company and what takeaway memories you are trying to create. Make sure that every bit of your event reflects your corporate image, symbolizes how your business is run, and displays your personal style.

TYPES OF BUSINESS EVENTS

"The number one unwritten rule of success is networking."
Sallie Krawcheck

By dint of the face-to-face contact they offer, events are eminently useful in business. A business event is an effective low-cost marketing method for developing sales opportunities and contacts. No other form of marketing offers such close personal communication and large-scale networking opportunities. Let's talk about some of the different types of events you can organize to benefit your business.

Business Meetings

Meetings are the most basic type of event in business. However, given the time we spend in them, they can be counterproductive when they are not organized properly. The better prepared the participants turn up, the more effective a meeting is likely to be. Be clear who will chair the meeting and who the attendees will be. Send out invites well in advance. Let the participants have the agenda in advance as well.

Conferences

Whether it is an internal one for your colleagues or an external one for customers or other participants, a conference needs to be imaginative and stimulating. It is important to understand what the participants at a conference expect to achieve and to make them feel that the time they spent has been productive.

A conference has to be organized in a manner that makes every session effective. The most usual components of a conference event benefiting business are the following:

Plenary Session

The plenary session, usually slotted at the beginning of the conference, is a good way of communicating with all participants at the same time. Consider carefully who will host the plenary session, and keep it short and focused.

Seminars

Following the plenary session, a conference usually breaks into seminars on various subjects that the conference is addressing. Seminars usually have designated speakers and are less interactive than breakout sessions. Delegates generally have a choice of which seminar they want to attend. Generally, ask delegates to book in advance so that you have an idea of the numbers expected at each seminar and can organize accordingly.

Breakout Groups / Workshops

Most conferences split the delegates into smaller groups that get together in different rooms at the venue. This is a good way to have the right people focus on various themes during the conference as well as to allow interaction between people of different backgrounds. Make sure that you have enough content to be addressed in order for the breakout groups to be productive.

Team Building

A team building session is usually a necessary component of an internal conference. Pick a pleasant activity that is not only fun but also enables people to communicate, solve problems together, and build mutual trust. Consider your audience profile to make an appropriate choice of activity.

Networking Opportunities

Networking is an important part of any conference. Often, for a large business, an annual conference is the only occasion for its managers to meet people who are based in different locations. Networking events can be either cocktails or meals, or other informal social events that allow people to interact and hold conversations.

Exhibitions / Trade Shows

An exhibition can be a part of a conference or a standalone affair. It brings together people around a common interest in an environment that facilitates display and communication. Exhibitions can be either internal or external.

For external exhibitions, most often you would look to display at an existing exhibition rather than organizing an entire exhibition on your own. Using the space at an exhibition is an effective way to display your product or services to a large audience. When booking a space, think about traffic flow and where people are likely to flock and spend the most time.

Marketing Drives

Businesses regularly launch marketing drives or products. These occasions can be scheduled with a larger event like a conference or a trade show, or planned as standalone events. Press coverage and PR are key to their success. Marketing drives aimed at creating high-level awareness of the product and its service coverage generally precede all-out advertising.

Award Ceremonies

Award ceremonies offer huge potential for creativity and punch. The ceremony can be for an industry, a chamber of commerce, or your own company. The idea is to reward the highest performers and inspire others to emulate them. Find someone who is highly respected by the recipients and the audience alike to present the awards.

Sports Events

While businesses often sponsor them, sports events are less usual for businesses to organize (unless the business is part of the sports industry). Sports events thrive on competition and community. Make sure you can cope with capacity expectations.

Celebratory Events

Celebratory events are put together to use an occasion—such as an anniversary, a milestone, or a publication—to create a community event and to highlight an achievement or an aspect of culture. Your decision to organize this kind of event is usually driven by your objectives and budget provisions.

A literary festival generally attracts a niche audience. Think about how to get the local business involved in your festival.

Food festivals are a great opportunity to rally your target audience around a theme that everyone can relate to and savor.

Performing Arts Events

If you are thinking of organizing a music, comedy, dance, or drama festival, begin by asking yourself if you know the right people or how you can get to them. You will need some big names to draw in the crowd you aim to get. Substance and atmosphere are pivotal for the success of such festivals. Artists and their managers have to view your event as important for them.

Road Shows

Road shows are a traditional discipline. These are events that are usually organized by the distribution or sales team rather than the marketing team. Here interactivity with likely buyers is the key, face-to-face interaction is the focus, and a brand or product is introduced in an engaging and convincing manner. The audience for these shows is limited but carefully selected, comprising potential buyers or distributors.

PROACTIVE PLANNING

"The beginning is the most important part of the work."
Plato

Begin with Brainstorming

Before you develop an event plan, hold a brainstorming session with your internal event network and your external marketing advisors. Look around your company and select people who will be engaged with your event to attend. Limit the participants in the brainstorming session; it makes sense to communicate only with decision makers who can own the ultimate result. Ask some intense purpose questions to guide your program to align your strategic and creative objectives.

Choose Your Message

In my personal experience I have seen that companies, especially small and medium-sized ones, often focus on discharging the wrong messages to their target market. For example, harping on about how good their product or service is rather than elaborating how it makes the customer's life better or safer. Constantly ask what message will positively impact your target market.

Develop an Overview

Create an executive summary that sets the tone for your program. Start with the reason why you are participating in the event in the first place. Include details about the big picture, such as main speakers, entertainment, educational value, and networking and socializing opportunities. Where possible, rephrase any existing content in line with the purpose.

If you are sponsoring a conference, seminar, or trade show, go to its website and see how you can use the information that is already available. Understand the purpose of the event for its target audience. However, never cut and paste the text for your use. Read and understand it and then rewrite it, in a manner suitable to your company, to use when you assemble your event plan. Find contact information and speak to the show producer's sales representative. Most often, they can provide you with a wide array of literature that you can use to tailor your event marketing plan.

Events as a Marketing Tool

Good marketing practices go a long way in deriving results from your events. Place events at the top of your marketing chain. It is from your marketing repertoire that you will be able to distil the right event strategy.

How does this event benefit your sales/marketing plans in terms of brand awareness, lead generation, relationship reinforcement, and market perception? Based on the answer to that question, what are your primary objectives for the event and what is the profile of your target audience? What marketing opportunities can you make use of at the event, for example, speaker, panel discussion, sponsorship, advertising, direct marketing, media coverage?

It's All about Relationships

Organizing great events is not just about spending money. In today's market, creatively using your money will get more value out of your events. The primary objective of most events is marketing. Events are an opportunity for you to establish a personal rapport to ensure smooth communication throughout the progress of a client or stakeholder relationship. Imagine how much time you will need to get on the schedule of an executive to ask certain basic questions, compared to getting some face time with the same person at an event.

Your relationship building at your event must include the following:

- Cultivate relationships at the right levels of seniority to reduce sales time.
- Promote your message face to face to your prospective customers.
- Discover the needs and concerns of your industry, customer base, and experts.
- Position your business as an industry leader in certain aspects or products.

If you do meticulous homework, it will bring you additional perspectives and ideas. You may even end up planning your event quite differently from your preliminary notions. Doing your homework is what brings your event value and differentiation.

PLANNING FOR SUCCESS

"Give me six hours to chop down a tree and I will spend the first four sharpening the axe."
Abraham Lincoln

Select a Suitable Date

Selecting a date is a major decision in planning your event. This goes a long way in ensuring the success of your event. When will the highest number of invitees be able to attend? What else is going on at the same time that might impact your event? Look at your target audience, the people who will make up your guest list. Be aware of any event in the city that may be competing for the same people.

Keep an Eye on the Calendar

Are there holidays, like Halloween, for instance, that might interfere? If you expect people to turn out as a family, then a school night is not good timing. Timing closer to exams will not be conducive for children to attend. In the evenings immediately after festivities, such as Christmas or New Year, people are generally tired and not keen to attend more functions. If you plan your event in the peak season, good venues will need to be booked more than a year in advance. Watch out for rain or snowstorm forecasts as well.

Organizing an event during school breaks, especially in March, can be poor timing. People are likely to be away. Long weekends should also be avoided. Guests may have chosen to extend their time off and it will reduce your attendance. People look forward to long weekends and often make plans well in advance. The evening of the first working day after a long weekend is also a bad time, because people may need to rest or catch up on certain things after a long weekend away.

Watch out for sports events. A clash with the NHL playoffs, for example, can be detrimental to the attendance at your event.

Time of the Week and Day

The day of the week and the time of day also play an important role in the success of your event. You have to know, for instance, where your participants will be coming from. If they are coming directly from the office, then an early dinner or cocktail reception is better than an affair that starts late in the evening.

Friday evenings are a poor choice for any official affair. A Friday lunch should also end before participants' minds become preoccupied with the weekend traffic. For corporate events, midweek, and for galas, a Saturday evening is the best for achieving high attendance. For a black-tie event during the week, allow your guests enough time to go home and change before they are expected to turn up.

Create a Checklist

- Develop a checklist, with target dates and the person responsible for each item, and continue to update it along with projected costs and payments made.
- Organizing a successful event requires careful planning and attention to detail. Check periodically to make sure that everything is on target.

- As soon as you have finalized the plans, create a team to organize the event as envisaged.
- The target dates for various steps involved must be adhered to.
- Be mindful of all of the deadlines. For example, deadlines for confirming the final number of guests or of hotel bookings.
- Create a function sheet enumerating each step of the way, from start to end, along with contact details of all the players.
- As you prepare function sheets, you will get to know how many people you will need for each task. The function sheets are information guides that inform your suppliers of the details of how you want your event to be organized.
- Each player has to know what their role is and when to chip in. Make it clear to your contractors and staff that what you have asked for is what you expect to see on the day of the event.
- Have everything finalized the day before the set-up starts, so that your team has time to cope with any last-minute challenges.

On the Event Day

- Let the contractors know who, from your team, will be supervising what on the day of the event, and what time they will arrive.
- The overall visual effect is important. That is how the people will see the event and how the camera will capture it.
- The next important thing is the ambience you create for your guests. Be mindful of fine details such as temperature, sound volume, and the amount of lighting. (We will discuss these in more detail later in the book.)

2. STRATEGY

BUSINESS EVENT STRATEGY

*"The essence of strategy is choosing
what not to do."*
Michael Porter

Marketing continues to be transformed by technology. One-on-one marketing has given way to online marketing, and ever-hipper online marketing means continue to emerge. There are efficient testing and measuring methodologies for assessing the comparative and absolute efficacy of marketing campaigns using the internet and media. Events, though, serve a greater purpose. Events are a way of opening communication or building a relationship with someone. They bring you interaction with and feedback from your target market. Events are the quickest means to reach a carefully chosen audience in a deliberate setting.

No matter the size of a company, it is important to put together an event strategy that includes hosting, sponsoring, or attending events. Discerning which of these best suits your business in a situation is an important decision. When appropriately planned and executed, events can be an extremely effective marketing tool. A well-administered event is an investment in the future. However, an event is never an isolated occurrence. In order to be productive, it has to go together with the company's overall marketing strategy.

Today there are so many tools available and various alternatives that make a case for your marketing dollars. Therefore, you have to be clear about what you want your event strategy to achieve for your business. It is meticulous attention and preparation of every step that differentiates a great event from an ordinary one. Here are some points to bear in mind while devising the event strategy for your company.

- Create an event strategy that best suits your business—its goals, means, strengths, products, and target market.
- Avoid the herd instinct; just because most people in your industry are participating in an event does not necessarily make it the best fit for you.
- Also, in our fast-changing times, an event that worked extremely well five years ago may no longer have the same market pull.
- Look at your sales plans and business goals before you start to define what events you will target to host, sponsor, or attend.
- Time your events to match the launch of major marketing initiatives, such as new products or customer announcements.
- Focus on the entire experience of your target audience—from the first point of contact with your team, your brand, and your products until the post-event follow-up. Engineer the perception at every step.
- Plan and execute your events around what makes you unique and delivers value to your customers.
- Track the achievement of objectives from your event in the form of face time with a selected audience, starting relationships, feedback on products, leads, new sales, and general perception.

The Decision to Sponsor

Your decision to sponsor or run a booth or a show at an event should be driven by the value-added marketing opportunities it brings to you. It must also lead to economic profit for your business—through a boost in sales, in image, or in recognition—as conference organizers usually end up making good money from sponsorship fees and so on.

Sponsorship can involve opportunities for prominent advertisement both onsite and online, as well as affiliate marketing, access to event attendee lists, hosting or attending hospitality functions, speaking slots, and press releases. Think clearly about what your company brings to the event you are participating in. In terms of market context, is it the right platform to present your products or services?

Let's now look at some of the most common types of events and the role they can play in your marketing strategy.

- **Trade Shows**

Trade shows are an effective tool for generating sales, as well as for enhancing recognition of your products and your brand. In order to leverage this tool well, a great deal of thought has to be put into selecting the right trade shows and planning the details. The first question is, will you reach the target audience?

- **Seminars**

Seminars are often useful in industries such as financial services, advisory, technology, and so on. Make sure that your seminar's agenda is a big draw for the target audience. If you are hosting a seminar, be sure to complement it with a meal or a cocktail before or after. This provides networking opportunities and enables further discussions and relationship building.

- **Conferences**

Conferences are a good opportunity for executive participation. These events provide interaction with peers as well as buyers. Hosting a conference is your company's opportunity to set the stage for your leadership. Other ways of using a conference as a part of your event strategy could be co-sponsorship or participation in business and hospitality sessions.

- **Road Shows**

Road shows are meant to launch new products, services, or transactions. Provided you have a robust selling proposition, road shows can be highly effective. They provide multifaceted coverage through speaking, exhibition, hospitality, publicity, direct marketing, and public relations.

- **Exhibitions**

Exhibitions are usually industry events in which you can participate as a sponsor, an exhibitor, or an attendee. They are ideal for presenting innovative or next-generation solutions.

- **Roundtables**

Roundtables provide a unique relationship-building atmosphere; you can use them to reach senior executives from your target market and partners. They should be white service events hosted in a first-class location.

- **Meetings**

Meetings are generally used to engineer peer-to-peer interaction to make or validate decisions. Meetings can be external (e.g., annual general meeting) or internal (e.g., executive off-site).

- **Online Events**

Hosting online events (webinars, video-conferences, and so on) is a great opportunity to educate people about your products or services without pulling them out of their offices.

- **Meals/Hospitality**

Use meal functions as valuable networking opportunities without featuring an explicit sales pitch. You can often host a hospitality event by piggybacking on another conference or trade show. You can also host hospitality events—such as cultural shows or musical programs—for pure entertainment.

- **Sports Events**

Consider sports events to bring your target audience together, for example, a golf tournament involving executives from your target market.

SHAPING YOUR STORY

"Think like a wise man but communicate in the language of the people."
William Butler Yeats

As you set about creating your event's message, you need to determine who you want your event to address and what message you want to communicate. Begin by looking at the event from your target audience's point of view to understand what will constitute a great experience for them. Let's talk briefly about how you can establish who your target audience is and how you can effectively communicate with them across an array of events.

Create an Identity

First and foremost, have a clear objective for the event in mind. Then focus on creating an event identity before you delve into the specific messages to be communicated to the audience. For example, if it is a sales event with a goal of creating new customers, your challenge will be to convince a targeted portion of your audience. The rest of the planning will revolve around this primary objective. Build an event plan that checks all your content and experience.

Events that you organize need to reflect your brand in the right light. But in addition, every event has its own brand that you should be able to communicate to its target market. Depending on the nature of the event and your own objectives, decide to what extent you want to build the event identity. For example, at many highly popular events—exhibitions, conferences, music festivals—most people don't know who the organizer is, but the event still achieves its purpose for the organizers.

Consider the message you want to communicate, how to bring it to life before the event, and how to keep it alive afterwards as well. When you have to include several brands in your experience messaging, organize the brands into an order in accordance with the event's primary objective. In order to ensure a consistent brand message, establish clear brand guidelines for your event team that sets broad rules about what can be done and what can't be done.

Ascertain Audience Awareness

As you shape your message for the event, consider how much your audience already knows and understands. For example, if they fully understand the product the event is promoting, then your message needs to focus on "why us?" instead of regurgitating things that the audience already knows. Even in communicating the "why us?" message, if your brand already has equity with the audience, then you need to focus less on brand awareness and more on product awareness: What is this product's merit over its competition?

Develop Your Message

Once you understand your target audience's awareness gap, you can then focus on what to tell them. For example, you may choose your message to focus straightaway on what distinguishes your offering from the competition's or from your own previous version of the same product or service.

Larger corporations, in particular, may also need to include the company's wider, strategic message. This part offers great opportunities for up-selling or cross-selling. It allows you to prioritize the action invoked in line with the sequence of the communication.

Once you have established the priority order of the communication, think about the tenor, language, and syntax in which your message needs to be communicated to its intended audience. For example, if you are targeting young people, do not preach to them. They will be a lot more receptive to something that is projected as highly appealing to their peer groups. Also, any idea that renders their social networking easier is an instant hit with youth today.

Build the Content

Content is the most important factor in the experience you create for your audience. An event generally has several types of content. Work closely with your event team to achieve a clear, common understanding of what you want your guests to experience at and after the event. Depending on how much variety there is, you may have different teams working on different parts of the content. All content that is created should be in line with the brand guidelines established for the event. Your choice of content will always be guided by who your audience is and what the venue offers. Some of the generic types of content are the following:

- **Slides:** Slides shown on a screen are one of the most common ways to communicate the message. They also serve well as prompts for presenters. Check the screen size that will be used and match your slides to it. Keep your slides brief and allow the audience sufficient time to read them. Use images, charts, and graphics to convey your message. Slides are easy to use and can be amended up until the last minute.
- **Video:** Videos are becoming increasingly popular and easy to use. Videos afford you a lot of room for creativity to make

your message unforgettable. Like slides, format your video in accordance with the screen.
- **Booklets and Other Printed Material:** It is a common practice at events to provide the guests with some handouts that they can take with them. Producing high-quality print content requires a significant investment of time.
- **Experiential Activity:** Events targeting consumers usually make use of interactive experiences. Your team must be creative to find engaging ways for the audience to get involved. Engaging the audience's interest is much more important than creating technically advanced content for interactivity.
- **Radio Frequency Identification (RFID):** Radio frequency identification can also be used to track a guest's experience at your event. It involves inserting smart chips into gift passes or wrist bands. You can install interactive screens at your event so that a sensor can detect each guest's chip to give them access to personalized, relevant information. As visitors scan in and out of each of the event's experiences, you can track their journey and gauge their interest to make improvements to their experience. However, the use of RFID for an event is expensive, as it entails acquiring both software and hardware.
- **Projections:** To project images onto a stage, be sure to use a ceiling-mounted projector so that the guests' movement does not block the projection. Projections are quite popular, and you can also add a soundtrack to them. Some of the common types of projections include 3D holographic video projections, fog screen projections, and video mapping.
- **Fireworks:** At the right moments, fireworks can lend both drama and impact to your event! Make sure that you have the necessary permits and insurance coverage for the fireworks display you envisage.

EXHIBITING THOUGHT LEADERSHIP

"Thought leadership is a way to build a relationship with prospects based on knowledge—not on products and services."
Chris Koch

A thought leader is an acknowledged leader in their field. What distinguishes a thought leader from any other expert or knowledgeable company is a broad recognition from the outside world that the company is always ahead of the curve in its industry. Companies today market thought leadership based on their expertise, knowledge, and a vanguard mind-set. Events do not create thought leaders, they exhibit thought leadership. Thought leadership is not about a sales pitch, it is about vision and ideas. Thought leaders are ambassadors for your company.

Events provide you access to a community where you can be identified as a thought leader. For each circle—customers, partners, employees, media, analysts—you can identify someone to represent your company as the chosen thought leader. Research, expertise, insight, knowledge, and vision are what make an individual a thought leader. The people you designate should be at the forefront and able to live up to what they profess. Their charisma and knowledge invigorate the brand image. The individual who is recognized as a thought leader can lift your sales and your brand recognition.

Every company has its own personality with business leaders and subject matter specialists. Events are an opportunity to leverage such individuals within your company to advance your message. It takes some work to ascertain who in your company can be used for public speaking, gatherings, and schmoozing. Thought leaders in your company are evangelists that you must know how to deploy in live environments. Most companies have both internal thought leaders (board members, founders, experts) and external ones (analysts, enthusiastic customers, writers, speakers) available to them. Through them, events afford your company a platform to talk about more than just your products. They give you an opportunity to talk about significant developments in your industry and your target market. Any time you get a speaking engagement, it is a chance to address the issues and present your vision.

Secure Speaking Engagements

Stud your events strategy with speaking engagements. At a business gathering, the quality of speakers is the first area that people look at to decide whether or not to attend. Speaking engagements are often a major reason for a company to host its own event. Identify the events that your customers or industry leaders are attending, and get on panels or lead workshops at them. Focus on providing useful information, as people haven't turned up to hear about your products or services. Use the opportunity to educate and articulate a unique outlook.

Here are some steps to securing a speaking engagement for your company.

1. Identify the people you can present as thought leaders to the managers of an event.
2. Develop a marketing piece in the guise of a bio, explaining why conference organizers should select your thought leader to speak.

3. Prepare a précis that addresses the subjects of the conference to find the topic that best matches your repertoire.
4. Call conference organizers to get their insight on what their audience really wants to hear, based on their experience or plans.
5. Involve your thought leaders early on to make sure that you book a slot on their calendar.
6. Make sure people turn up. Confirm and reconfirm. Work with your sales and PR people to get the target audience in attendance.
7. Brief the thought leader thoroughly on your key messages, and provide the reference material in advance. Create a briefing kit.
8. Where appropriate, boost the speaking engagements with a special offer or a promotional item.

Press and analyst relations go a long way in promoting your thought leadership. To determine which individuals are important for an event, assess the topics being covered and their tone with the press and analysts. Take advantage of the media list the conference organizer generates. Schedule meetings with journalists and analysts in advance and extend the discussion.

Treat press and analysts as you would treat your top customers: cultivate relationships with them. Invite them to a private VIP dinner and lure them with exclusive meetings with senior executives. Preparation is critical. Set up pre-briefings; putting unprepared customers or executives in front of press and analysts can be counterproductive. Content is a part of an event that is hard to deliver. You can drive publications to have the editors provide you with a voice, and show the best of what your company offers.

Get Recognized

Finally, let's briefly discuss how one becomes acknowledged as a thought leader. It starts with being open with what you know and being generous with your time and knowledge. Here are some of the steps involved in becoming established as a thought leader:

- **Build Relationships with Media:** Have a list of media people who cover your industry and marketplace. Make sure you call them and meet with them from time to time. Help them with leads, insight, or stories.
- **Write:** Write pieces that have useful information for your target market. Write articles, whitepapers, and so on, to show that you understand the issues of your industry and have suggestions to solve them. Be generous with your expertise.
- **Get Published:** Use the press, your website or blog, and so on.
- **Do Public Speaking:** Find opportunities to address trade shows, conferences, and seminars. Get on panels. Lead workshops.
- **Make Your Website Useful:** Use your website for active and informative exchange of knowledge. The more useful information your website has, the more it will be linked to.
- **Make Thought Leadership a Priority:** You do not need to have a dominant market share in order to reach out to the market with useful ideas. Look at your company from an outsider's perspective and see whose insight or expertise can be useful to establish thought leadership credentials.

3. TARGET MARKET

DETERMINING YOUR TARGET AUDIENCE

"When you align your message with what people are already passionate about, you are able to make an emotional connection."
Tim Burke

Within your target market, your target audience is the one to whom your message at the event is directed. Who you want to have at your event is based on what they do in their companies or businesses. Generally speaking, these people fulfil one or more of three roles for you: advocates, enablers, or customers. Each member of your target audience has different characteristics in relation to your sales strategy.

Think about all the personal touches that can set your events apart and thus enhance your sales strategy. Multiple touchpoints are the key differentiators in the success of an event. During the event cycle, there will be several opportunities to connect with each member of your target audience. At a successful event, that interface is meaningful and resonates with the target audience.

Determine the Audience Profile

Getting your target audience to your event is your first challenge. It starts with determining the profile of your target audience and then identifying people who match it. I have learnt in a long corporate career that there are only so many types of industries and so many people within those industries. Often roles within an organization overlap or are shared. Each industry has its list of roles and titles. Take a look at the top events that are hosted in that industry to research their content, presentation, and attendees.

Involve Sales People

To ascertain the target audience for your event, begin by talking to your sales people. The ultimate objective of a business event is to connect your sales force with your target market. Identify and involve the sales people responsible for the relevant markets and seniority levels. The buy-in of your sales people is essential for an event's success. Get executive backing from sales early on and work with your sales people to identify the industries and people that you need to have attend your event to meet its objectives. The sales force is also a valuable resource for marketing your event, allowing you to overcome access and personality issues. Whether it is a trade show, a golf tournament, a gala, or an executive meeting, the sales people's live performance is highly important. Marketing that is not aligned with sales is pointless. Therefore, a collaborative sales and marketing relationship must be constantly nurtured.

Events are a tremendous opportunity for the sales people to directly reach their customers and channels. By involving sales in your event strategy, you also add to the account-based marketing perspective. Account-based marketing is about establishing relationships around a customer account, where the movement of individuals within or leaving their organization does not make much difference to the B2B relationship. It allows you to go deep with the company. You have several contacts at various seniority levels within that account. You then have account-wise sales objectives in addition to product or solution centered goals. Understand your customers' organizational structure to target the right players.

Include Other Business Segments

You have to be discerning in your treatment of various segments of your target audience. These may include the following:

Chief Guests, Top Executives, and Board Members:

Understand the hierarchical dynamics to be able to look after executives well. There is generally enough information available on these people for you to build familiarity for highly skillful handling. They expect white-glove service.

Senior to Middle Management:

Management is critical for conducting day-to-day business with their entities. Making them look good in the eyes of their superiors will help you create embedded relationships with them.

Sponsors:

Build relationships with sponsors, but be wary of sponsors that are targeting the same market as you.

Other Stakeholders:

For other stakeholders, it is more about educating them to better understand your business. Sometimes a more embedded relationship may be required.

Once you have profiled your target audience, you have to know what your goals are for an event and how its success will be measured. In order to be able to impact the bottom line, your sales people have to be able to follow up to establish relationships or conduct transactions.

SHAPING THE EVENT FOR YOUR AUDIENCE

"There is only one winning strategy. It is to carefully define the target market and direct a superior offering to that target market."
Philip Kotler

In business, you organize events to reach out to various target audiences. These could be other businesses, your customers, or even your employees. Once you have determined who exactly your target audience is, you will find it a lot easier to design your event. Your target audience determines both the type of event you want to organize as well as its content. It is difficult to interest everyone through one event. Hence, if you have a broad target market, you have to be clear which part of your target market you want an event to appeal to. Depending on the purpose of the event, it is possible to use one event to communicate with more than one group of audiences, but you have to craft the content accordingly.

Be Meticulous

Once you have identified a target market group, you need to be more specific about the profile of the audience you want to attract from within that group—gender, age, income level, ethnicity, education level, family structure, interests and hobbies. Where possible, try to test your ideas about the event against a representative group of your target audience. For example, if you are planning a major internal party, it will be useful to form a steering group of people of different ages from different departments.

Scan the Competition for Ideas

Looking at the events organized by your competition is a good place to begin developing your own ideas. Knowing what competitors are offering their customers, partners, or employees will give you an idea of what does and does not appeal to your target market. Don't just copy, do better. Most business attendees are keen to know what level of people from the industry will attend. Use your loyal and influential customers or partners as the emissaries for the event. Ask them if they are willing to play a more participative role in the event.

Use Data for Recurring Events

Some of the events you organize may have a captive audience or a large number of people who have attended earlier editions. For recurring events, you already have the data and knowledge of the previous attendees to start with. If they had a good experience previously, then convincing them to attend is easier than getting new guests to join. It may help to send them photos from the previous event to remind them of the good time they had. Keep in mind that people who have previously attended already have an expectation and will look forward to the event being better than the previous one.

Communicate Effectively

Even when attendance is almost obligatory—for employees, for example—in order to get the most out of your event, you still need to communicate in advance what the event will be about and what they can expect to help achieve. Quality communication prior to the event will ensure that they turn up enthused and prepared.

4. THE VENUE

LOCATION, LOCATION, LOCATION

"It's all about the location."
Stephany Sofos

Selecting the right location for your event is of paramount importance. You need to match your site to the type of event, while ensuring it is convenient and accessible to your guests. Begin with an overview of your event and note all your requirements, for example, dressing rooms for entertainers, an area to prepare displays, or a cozy place for the bride to wait in. Imagine all the space requirements for the type of event you are organizing. Establish a preliminary cost sheet and then start investigating the possible venues. Keep updating and amending the cost sheet as you progress.

Think of the Possibilities

Don't feel limited to restaurants, hotels, or banquet halls. There are numerous other possibilities, some of them more unique. For example, a golf club, an art gallery, an airport hangar, a warehouse, a modish boutique, or setting up tents over a parking lot or a tennis court, or hiring a yacht. Guided by your objective and your budget, any suitable space can be taken over and transformed, constrained only by your imagination. What is important is to find the best fit within your budget. Discovering new venues and creating one-of-a-kind events is how you carve out memorable occasions. However, be aware of any restrictions. Art galleries, heritage buildings, and so on, have rules about what can take place there. For example, you may not be allowed to attach anything to the walls or to serve food in certain areas.

Access Time

While selecting a venue, be aware of what precedes your event. Be clear about the exclusive access time to the facility. Make sure that access time for decor and set-up has been clearly agreed. Do not feel limited by the furniture at the venue; most facilities are willing to remove furniture to create more space for your guests. Determine beforehand who will provide the cleaning crew. It cannot be taken for granted.

Noise Restrictions

Find out about any noise restrictions. If the facility is in the midst of a residential area, there are likely to be rules for how loudly music can be played and how late can your event last.

Food, Drinks, and Tableware

If it is a team building event and the guests are participating in some physical activities, serve alcohol after and not before the activity. Ask to take a look at the tableware that will be used to ensure that the china, the glassware, and the cutlery are up to the standard you expect. Good-quality utensils add to an event.

Venue Staff

Find out about the quality of the staff at the venue. How experienced are they? Have they handled events of this nature before? Ask the facility to provide you with their best and most professional people. Discuss important aspects of protocol with facility management so that they can apprise their staff accordingly. While efficiency is a constant, staff's demeanor and appearance have to complement the occasion.

Weather Forecast

When organizing an outdoor event, thoroughly check the weather forecast and, should there be slightest risk, keep a plan B readily at hand.

Paperwork

Review your contracts and function sheets with all concerned people to ensure that nothing has been overlooked. Have all your paperwork—permits, licenses, contracts—available at the time of your event so that you can deal with any concerns or disputes right away.

Disability Access and Inclusion

Make sure your event is accessible to all attendees by checking that the venue you select has disability and access inclusion features available. Make sure your event is accessible to wheelchair users and is also programmatically accessible to people with disabilities. This can be accomplished through provisions such as interpreters for people who are deaf, assistive listening devices or captioned videos for hearing impaired people, and large print, E-text, or Braille handouts of programs for visually impaired people. All registration materials and promotional stuff announcing events should state that your event is accessible to people with disabilities. It is suggested that you ask participants to request accommodations or identify their needs well in advance of the event, so that you can plan and recruit service providers to meet their needs. If no request has been made, you may not be required to provide special accommodations. You must, however, provide physical access to your event, ensuring that individuals with mobility impairments can attend.

HOW TO SELECT A VENUE

*"So much of difference between a triumph and a flop
is determined by choice of venue."*
Anatoly Belilovsky

Your choice of an event venue is of critical importance. Sometimes choosing a venue for your event can be simple, but it may also be very complex. In the previous chapter we discussed general factors to look at while considering a location. Now establish more detailed criteria to help you make your selection. Once you have established the right criteria, following them will bring you to your final choice. Do some research around the possible venues and make a shortlist of the ones that are likely to meet your expectations. When you are considering multiple venues, don't feel compelled to decide right away; instead, visit sites to better compare and deliberate.

Evaluate Your Choices

Normally, you should visit a few different sites before you choose a venue. Some aspects you may consider are the following:

- Does it fall within your budget?
- Is the venue large enough?
- Does it offer the right appearance and quality for the event?
- Is it conveniently accessible to your target audience?

Look at the Details

Once you have a preferred site, undertake a technical inspection. Some of the points you need to discuss with the venue manager are the following:

- the suppliers provided by the venue
- the staff provided by the venue
- any restrictions on the outside suppliers
- vehicle access, including cargo and parking
- audience access
- facilities on site, for example, kitchen, backroom, sound, lighting, power, toilets
- marketing and branding support
- exact floor space and capacity of the areas to be used for the event
- transport options
- internet access

Finally, put your agreement with the venue in writing. Read the contract provided by the venue thoroughly before signing it. It must detail all of the plans, deliverables, and costs. Keep an eye on any veiled add-on costs like management fees or corkage charges. Establish clear cancellation costs. Clarify any ambiguities before signing.

Types of Venues

Some of the common types of venues are as follows:

1. Permanent Facilities

You can choose from a large array of spaces tailored to host your event. Permanent facilities offer you the advantage of existing infrastructure and a trained team on the ground. They are usually also more economical than creating your own event space. Any suitable building can be an event space, but these are some of the typical types of permanent facilities:

- **Convention Centers**

    Convention centers normally offer huge floor areas including an auditorium, large halls, and meeting rooms. They also have all the expertise and resources in place to hold very large gatherings as well as smaller events. While considering a convention center for your event, find out what other events are taking place there at the same time. There could be events you may not want to clash with for any number of reasons.

- **Heritage Sites and Galleries**

    Venues with a telling story behind them usually make a great event space. Often they can complement the theme of your event. Normally such venues are in high demand and their managers can be very choosy.

- **Hotels**

    Most hotels have ballrooms and conference facilities. A hotel can provide you with a host of other facilities like lodging, parking, and catering. Hotels usually offer a high quality of service, but their setting is often fairly bland. You may need to add your own decoration and setting.

- **Sports Arenas**

    Sports and leisure arenas can also be used for non-sports events, as the infrastructure is already in place to accommodate large gatherings of people.

- **Malls**

    Shopping malls are highly frequented areas where large numbers of people turn up in a good mood and already willing to spend money. Most malls have large event spaces that generally make good venues for brand awareness or product launch events. They are also family-friendly venues. When planning an event at a mall, keep in mind its opening and closing hours as well the busier times of the day.

2. Outdoor Venues

An outdoor venue usually offers ample space to make use of without any pre-existing decor and style. Holding an event outdoors, though, may require a lot more work. Such sites are usually run by local city or town councils and are not too expensive to rent. However, obtaining approval from the council may take time, so the process should be started well in advance. Some things to consider if you choose a venue outdoors are the following:

- **Boundaries**

    If there are no natural boundaries, then marking your own can involve cost. Quite often the site may need to be fenced for reasons of security and control.

- **Security**

    When hosting an outside event, make sure your area is secure and fun. Be sure the space is large enough for the number of people you have in mind, and provide safety barriers where necessary. Also ensure that you have the necessary signage and first aid and safety support on site.

- **Water**

    Availability of water is often taken for granted by guests. Keep in mind the water supplies on the site, and be sure to arrange for routing or distribution to different areas as needed on the event day.

- **Power Supply**

    An outdoor venue may not have a permanent power supply. You may need to arrange for a generator.

- **Tents**

    You will most likely need to rent tents to put up your own structure to meet your space configurations and provide shelter from sun and rain. A wide variety of tents are available to transform your site into an event venue. Some tents have poles with a peak in the middle to create a marquee, whereas others are pole structures that use aluminum frames. You can choose whatever best suits the structure you want on the site. When deciding how big a tent you need, allow about 15 square feet (1.4 square meters) per person. A low-cost option for creating different rooms at your event is to use shipping containers for the purpose. At an outdoor event, you may also need to organize for temporary flooring. (We will discuss tents in more detail later.)

- **Weather**

    Weather is an important factor to consider when organizing an outdoor event. Make sure you have arrangements in place to shelter people from sun, rain, extreme temperatures, and strong winds.

- **Special Venues**

  If you are bringing a special theme to life or looking to do something distinctly memorable, you can go for an atypical venue. These can include barges and boats, building sites, museums, night clubs, or schools. Such venues offer their unique features, both negative and positive.

- **Destination Venues**

  There can be challenges in organizing events at destination venues, but meticulous planning can tackle those. If your budget allows, you can also partner with a destination management company to outsource the organization of your logistics as well as the event.

- **Road Show**

  Sometimes your event may involve several venues if your audience is based in different areas and you need to put up smaller events that are accessible in different places. You may want to customize your event a little bit to each venue. Such an event, in effect, is made up of several mini-events. Organizing logistics is an important part of planning a road show.

Make Your Own Venue

If you don't find a perfect venue for your event, you can also create your own. Creating your own venue may entail a lot more work, but it also affords you more flexibility to create a space that exactly matches your requirements. The event space you use can be as simple as a tent in a playground or something more elaborate, like a warehouse. When you organize an event in a place that is not a usual event space, it may require additional paperwork to get all necessary permissions in place.

SETTING UP A VENUE

"Form follows function."
Louis Sullivan

Think Before You Select

It is important to consider all of your set-up requirements before looking for a location for your event. In addition to the number of people and the seating arrangement you want, think of other details. Do you want rear-screen projection? Do you want a dance floor? Do you need storage space? Do the musicians or performers need a change room? What ceiling height and clear space are needed for the sightlines and the spectacle you desire? Will you need a blackout for a visual presentation? These are a few among many things to consider. Only when you have a complete wish list ready can you know what you can best get out of a venue and what compromises you are prepared to make.

The Room

You want a room that looks comfortably packed and vibrant, but not overcrowded. Faced with a choice between a slightly bigger and a slightly smaller room, go for the bigger one. You can always reduce its size through decoration. If you are using a portion of a larger ballroom, inspect it when it is fully empty with the air wall in place. See if noise from the other side of the partition can pose a problem. Try to set up staging in a manner that minimizes bad seats in the audience. Watch out for pillars and hanging chandeliers that disrupt the sightlines. Always optimize the floor plan. Ask the facility to provide a layout based on what you are looking for.

For a cocktail reception, you require about 9 square feet (0.84 m^2) per person, whereas for cocktails with food stations, you will need about 13 to 16 square feet (1.39 m^2) per person. For a seated dinner, look for about 21 square feet (1.95 m^2) per person. A dance floor is comfortable with about 3.5 square feet (0.33 m^2) per person. If you have a live band playing, then provide for about 20 square feet (1.86 m^2) per instrument. For a formal sit-down dinner, seat 8 people on tables of 10, and 10 people on tables of 12. Make sure that tables are not too close together to hamper easy movement.

Check if the room has the type of floor you are looking for. You can transform any floor to conform to your needs. If you need a dance floor, how big does it need to be? Also consider whether you want air walls to be in place for a part of your event and then removed. Are they manual or powered?

Decide on how the room will be set up. Is it a plated dinner or a buffet, or will food be passed around? Think of the seating accordingly. For example, you could have people seated in designated places, or have them stand with some scattered seating available.

Make sure that tear-down of any adjacent events at the facility does not coincide with the timing of your event. You don't want hammering or packing noise while your event is still going on.

The Stage

If your event involves a stage, will it be a revolving one? Will you require ramps? Make sure that the decor of your stage works with what will be taking place on the stage. Coordinate with all of your suppliers to ensure your staging requirements. Also consider if your stage area will require draping.

Entertainment

If your event includes a live performance, find out if a rehearsal is required by the performers and for how long. Make time and space available accordingly. Similarly, find out how much time will be needed to set up the audiovisual requirements. Where possible, it is better to have a single supplier that can cater to your needs for audiovisual, lighting, and staging. Spend more money on what is essential for the success of your event. For example, you may need only a simple stage but an absolutely top-notch audiovisual set-up. Likewise, in music programs, light effects may be essential in some but less important in others. Focus your efforts around what best fits your needs and not what is easily available or nice to have.

Special Effects

Find out from the facility if they offer any special effects that you can use. Even restaurants often offer special effects such as special lighting, laser shows, waterfalls, and so on. Also find out if there are any restrictions on indoor fireworks, laser shows, or any other special effects you have in mind.

USING TENTS

"I think our big tent is our greatest strength."
Tom Perez

Tents can be used creatively at your event, either as the main venue or as additional space. A tent can also provide shelter and shade in case of inclement weather. Consider what type of tent is best suited for your needs. Contact local tent rental companies and take a look at the types of tents they supply. Make it clear to them that the tents they install must not have scratches, stains, or cracks. Similarly, a tent with a dirty sidewall is an eyesore. You don't want your supplier to be cleaning the tents as the guests start coming in. You can also choose from different types of sidewalls. If you expect warm weather with a refreshing breeze, sidewalls that can roll up will allow in fresh air while a lining of mesh stays in place to keep insects out.

Site Inspection

It is important to get your tent supplier to do a site inspection at your venue to determine what type and size of tent will best suit your event. Terrain will need to be examined and accurate measurements taken. It is important that the tent design works with your location. The supplier will also need to see if the tent can be set in the ground or if it requires anchoring equipment. If there are permanent trees in the area, the ceiling of the tent must be higher than the trees. Also determine how strong the impact of wind is in the area. Is it in a wind tunnel or at a ridge crest? If the site is uneven or the ground is damp, then a floor is a must.

Permissions

Consider the necessary permits and permissions you will need in the place where you are setting up the tent. You may need permission from the owner of the land or a tent permit or a hydro permit. If warranted, see how your tent needs to be set up to comply with the alcohol-serving regulations of your area.

Catering Needs

You also need to ascertain the caterers' needs. If they are cooking inside the tent, it will require sufficient aeration; you will need to install an appropriate exhaust system. You will also need to provide for your caterers' illumination and electrical requirements. How will you meet your electricity and water requirements? Do you have access to connections, or will you rely on makeshift arrangements? These are important details that must be spelled out in the relevant contracts.

Budget for All Costs

Make a detailed budget that also accounts for all anticipated extra costs. For example, the site may involve rental charges, or you may need to set up a separate tent for cooking. Do you need to arrange for portable restrooms or rent bathroom trailers? Also build into your budget the extra cost for security to guard the tent overnight before and after your event. Ascertain whether or not clean-up charges need to be provided for separately. Also determine if you need to make heating arrangements or set up air-conditioning.

It's always a good idea to get your supplier to set up your tent a day before your event.

5. MARKETING

ALL ABOUT PUBLICITY

"The sole purpose of business is service. The sole purpose of advertising is explaining the service which business renders."
Leo Burnett

Get the Word Out

Unless you know what goes into publicizing events, you are not likely to get the desired turnout. Creating a publicity campaign around an event is a lot of fun and can summon every bit of ingenuity you have. Effective publicity makes use of both traditional methods and social media tools. Depending on the nature of your event, you can either have a pre-decided guest list or a public event with a target audience in mind. The latter demands a more intensive publicity campaign. The publicity must communicate the following information: date and venue, agenda, cost of attendance, any measures attendees should take before arriving, general event and brand awareness for those who are not attending. The publicity campaign of an event, generally, has three stages:

- **Prior to the Event:** At this stage, you publicize the purpose of the event, mainly to the target audience.
- **At the Event:** You try to stretch the reach of the event well beyond the people who are physically present.

- **Following the Event:** At this stage, you leverage the event to create brand awareness and to continue a relationship with the attendees.

In this chapter, I will focus on the pre-event publicity that starts with the creation of a marketing plan.

Make a Marketing Plan

The marketing plan for your event should cover the following:

1. **Information About the Target Market:** Whom do you intend the event and its publicity to target? Ascertain what your target market thinks and how they react to your publicity techniques.
2. **Overview of the Event:** Include basic information about what your event consists of. Describe your event in a way that not only enables people to attend, but also makes them want to. The description should be short, leaving people wanting to find out more.
3. **Event Objectives:** What is your main purpose for the event? What are the key performance indicators to measure its success?
4. **Event Publicizing Strategy:** How do you plan to reach out to your target market to ensure they know about your event? Start by deciding a media strategy, including social media and traditional media. A lot of effective publicity, these days, can be done for a minimal cost with a bit of imagination. For many events, you may not even need paid media, especially with good PR. Create a brand identity for your event that includes the following:

    - **Name:** The name should be pertinent and easy to remember. Create an acronym for longer names.
    - **Perception:** Project what you want the guests to experience at your event.

- **Positioning:** Think of a catchy word or phrase to publicize your event, something that sounds like a rallying cry to the target audience.
- **Website:** Consolidate your content architecture on an event website or on a section or page on your company's website. Your website can serve as a hub for social action or it can merely be a source of information. These days you can set up a website on your own with a little help.
- **Social Media:** A large part of your event's target audience is online, as social media has become an integral part of our lives. Make social media a part of all your event publicizing plans, using tools that are important to your audience. Some popular platforms are Facebook, LinkedIn, YouTube, Pinterest, and Twitter. Whatever your choice of the social media, make sure that you have content that people want to share and conversations that people want to join.
- **Press Launch:** Hosting a press launch can be a cost-effective way to generate media coverage. Be sure to prepare a press pack for the launch that includes a fact sheet, a list of performers with their bios, a short profile of your business and any partners involved, and a brief history of the event. Follow up with all attendees to check if they need further information. Also issue a press release, where possible.
- **Blogging:** You can either create your own blog or use an established blogger on the subject.
- **Public Relations:** PR is useful in convincing others of the worth of your event, especially for external events that the general public, industry people, or media can attend. PR can also influence the press by cultivating relationships with journalists and proactively providing them with information.
- **Online Event Sites:** You can list your event on a number of online listing sites, many of which are free. These sites are frequently visited and can drive traffic to your event website.

- **Online Advertising:** The most effective tools for online advertising are Facebook and Google AdWords. Focus on the right demographic in the right location.
- **Conventional Advertisement:** Traditional modes of advertisement include radio, outdoor marketing, graffiti, road signs, mobile marketing, TV, press, and direct mail.

5. **Timing:** Plan your marketing to resonate with the timing of your event planning. Be aware of what else you are competing with at the same time as your event to capture your target market's attention and presence. Generally, in order for your marketing plan to be effective, begin three to four months before the event. Focus the main push of the marketing about one month before the event, when people are likely to be marking their diaries for the period during which your event is planned. Be aware of the relevant events leading up to yours; they are usually good opportunities to market your event. See if you can do some promotional activity at that point in time.

Whatever methods you choose, a targeted marketing approach is always better than doing a bit of everything. A marketing plan is not merely about determining what to do and when; it is more about ensuring that the whole action list comes together appropriately to build and execute a convincing and interconnected campaign.

BUILDING YOUR IMAGE

"Life isn't about finding yourself. Life is about creating yourself."
George Bernard Shaw

Events generate recognition for a business; they enable the business to show the market what products and services it has to offer. It is important to use events as a tool of your marketing repertoire. Business events can be classified into two broad categories: trade shows or conferences; and proprietary events hosted by you alone or by you and your partners in a venture. Events are primarily aimed at making connections, as they help you connect with your customers and other stakeholders on a human level—personalizing a business to its customers in particular. An event is an opportunity to establish or reinforce a relationship that can be followed up with a phone call or action.

Image building is not just about getting your brand out there. Your image is the story that your name or your brand invokes. It is not just the live environment that conveys your image, but also the minor details or logistics around your event.

If your input into your event is lacking, it is your own fault if the event does not meet your expectations. While overseeing events organization in my corporate roles, I would carefully review each touchpoint during the entire event cycle, making sure that everything from pre-event solicitation to onsite execution to post-event actions delivered the right image. This includes both explicit branding of your logo or your name and more discreet branding focused on the image you want to project.

Here are some tips on how you can use your events to communicate your image to the market:

Align with Your Business Objectives

No matter how well organized an event is, it can only be called successful if it is fully aligned with your business objectives and your sales initiatives. It is more relational than merely strategic, and it starts with talking, listening, and making contacts. Talk to the business leaders in your field and establish your objectives from a particular event in the context of your overall business plans.

Include Influencers

Think about and understand your business imperatives for communicating and interacting with your customers, your target market, your suppliers and distributors, and your staff. Pay close attention to media and market analyses. Engage people—they love to talk—and learn by asking questions. Find people within your organization who can champion your business at different forums and levels. They are your own event network.

Integrate with Marketing

Whether you work for a large corporation or a small business, marketing is about evangelizing, promoting, and backing your sales efforts. By integrating marketing into events, you are merely pushing the sales. Events would be a waste of money unless you get a return in sales. Your event must be aimed at adding vigor and recognition to your company's sales initiatives and business objectives. Clearly identify how an event strategy or an individual event will support the company's marketing initiatives and its PR drive. Once you understand this, you will have the context to use the power of events to fullest advantage.

Directly Engage Clients

Every event you undertake is a communication opportunity to show your business in the best light. Make sure that your event entails an active flow of information and integrates participants into the proceedings rather than treating them as passive attendees. When we engage clients at an event, the communication, positioning, program, optical signals, and the overall tenor must resound with the core objective that we have in mind.

Connect with Branding

It is up to you whether your event is a success in building the image you have in mind. Event planners are great at logistics, but are often not strategic; they only do a good job of delivering the pieces. Be sure that the event integrates your company's image, which can be a simple logo or a wide range of product brands. Image building, or brand recognition, is the primary objective of most business events. Branding is the main abiding connection between all your events, with each event branded to emphasize your image. Even companies with a strong market image need to work tirelessly to maintain their brand dominance and prestige.

MARKETING YOUR MESSAGE

"Marketing is no longer about the stuff that you make, but about the stories you tell."
Seth Godin

Once you decide to be part of an event and set about marketing it, the first thing you need to decide is what message your company wants to communicate to the target audience. You will have to be clear who your target audience at the event is, what you want to convey to them, and how your success will be measured. In order for your message to be effective, make sure that it is no longer than 30 words. Anything longer than that will never get through to your target audience in a live presentation environment where they are being bombarded with messages. Less is better.

In their book *How to Advertise*, Kenneth Roman and Jane Maas explain that a good marketing strategy must cover five key points:

1. **Objective:** What is your purpose in hosting the event or in participating in it?
2. **Target Audience:** What is the profile of the audience you are targeting?
3. **Benefit:** How does the target audience benefit from buying your product?
4. **Support:** What reason you can provide for the audience to believe in the benefit you have cited?

5. **Tonality:** Are the form and terminology of your message a statement of the product's personality?

An event is an opportunity to leverage your voice in a live environment. Do not start messaging the market until you have a brand. It is that brand that you want to get out there with consistency and punch. Only when you know what you want your brand to be can you determine positioning and messaging. Once you have the brand vision and know what you want to communicate, you are ready to decide how. The objective is to make emotional and practical connections among the brand, message, and audience. Find ways to touch the hearts of your audience; it is the emotional connection that will set you apart from your competitors.

Be sure what you say directly to your target audience at an event matches the overall positioning framework that is at the core of your company's branding. If necessary, circulate an event messaging document to the relevant departments or people within your company to elicit feedback. Then get consensus on the three main messages you want to convey at your event. Get a senior executive to present the message to your team; authority has people's ears.

Representatives from your company will interact with customers, prospects, partners, and media at the event. Make sure your team knows what to say and that they are given tools to communicate effectively, reinforcing the message of your speakers and advertising materials. The time you invest on the front end will come in handy when you complete the items needed for the event. Get the story straight, using customer testimonials and awards won by your company. Keep messages to a maximum of three and feature them throughout the event.

When it comes to the live event, find a strategic position in a booth located near the busiest area. Be consistent in the words you use for signage and banners and in the event program. Marketing is not just about telling a beautiful story but also about getting it remembered.

Creative event marketing has the power to make a brand memorable. Find ways to enhance the most compelling part of your story. Nothing communicates your brand better than a live scripted presentation with powerful visual support. It has to be short and filled with benefits. It has to be aimed precisely at your audience—neither above them nor below them. It has to be memorable and engaging, not necessarily entertaining. It has to be interactive—asking questions, provoking thoughts. The people handling or delivering the brand for you have to be skilled professionals.

If you have an executive thought leader who is an effective communicator, use her, where it is worth her time, to communicate your message at the events. A personal story from a senior voice will make your message much more powerful. It will be something completely individual, containing the corporate message, and delivered by an individual of some stature. Nothing builds rapport better than a leader who can communicate. Think, for example, of Bill Clinton, Ronald Reagan, or Barack Obama.

SALES TOOLS

"It's really the popularity with the target audience that counts."
Stephen Greyser

Events provide your business with a great opportunity for face-to-face networking with your target audience. You can feel the energy in the live environment, bringing people together for a shared purpose or activity, away from a formal work setting. In addition to face-to-face communication, it is also an opportunity to convey a message to the target audience through print or visual sales tools. Therefore, ensure that your tools reflect your brand and positioning and are assimilated into your event marketing repertoire. The content of sales tools should be consistent for print material, videos, websites, and downloads.

Once you have identified your target audience and established your event plan, it is time to decide what sales tools you need to distribute at the event. Plan details from content development and presentation to distribution and timing. Think of innovative ways to get your message out. Well-organized events, presenting your business and your products in the best possible light, go a long way in enhancing the efficacy of your sales tools.

Stay ahead of the curve in using technology in a fast-changing world. In the final analysis, it is all about the touchpoints. Sales tools are meant to be used. While deciding on sales tools, consider the target audience and think what they will like to bring home with them. Will they read the written word? What are they more likely to read? Stay on top of contemporary jargon and trends in your industry. Acronyms and buzzwords can be quite engaging at events.

There is no magic formula how each company provides sales tools at its events. Devise a combination of materials that is right for your sales initiatives and business goals. Here are some of the ideas for using sales tools at your events:

- The message should be in consonance with your image. Use appropriate tone and language to present an idea, and be concise.
- The material you develop must be easy for the sales force to use and convenient for the customer to read.
- Don't tell long stories, talk about advantages.
- Create a specific flyer or postcard for each event.
- Create a nice folder with the company logo to distribute material like brochures, testimonial flyers, and press coverage. Always tuck a sales rep's business card in the folder.
- If you distribute pen and pencil sets, use a branded ribbon and a gift bag with a logo.
- Find creative ways to promote a recent award your company has received.
- Create attractive table-top signs to display at your events.
- Don't be shy to use quotes from happy customers or favorable media coverage.
- Be selective in distributing costlier items. Set up clear criteria for the recipients.

Here are some of the sales tool items that you can choose from to match deliverables to your event cycle: website, calendars, email blasts, customer testimonials, direct mail, commercials, catalogues, CDs/DVDs, USBs, brochures, books, annual reports, article reprints, ad flyers, analyst reports, award announcements, presentations, product or service coverage sheets, folders, newsletters, and magazines.

GIVEAWAYS AND PROMO MATERIAL

"The new source of power is not money in the hands of a few, but information in the hands of many."
Jοhn Naisbitt

Promotional materials to be used at your event and the giveaways to be handed out to the guests are important tools to reinforce your message. During my years in management, I always viewed getting creative with our visual materials as a challenge. So can you. Every surface in your event is an opportunity to touch your target audience, a chance to bring your company's positioning and message to life. The visual material you create for an event is different from the giveaways and sales literature. Look at these items as your event decorations—decorations that lend beauty to the setting while identifying who you are and what you do.

In my experience, the events that top the list for getting the branding right are children's birthday parties. They almost invariably have the right theme, and all the materials—invitations, linen, hats, napkins, plates, giveaways—are consistent with the branding objective. Keep this an example in mind. The entire event cycle—online communications, PR, invitations, telephone calls, advertising, the onsite program, and follow-ups—should be used to maximize the brand.

You have to be able to leverage the creativity and cost incurred in what you produce not just once but at multiple business events. There also has to be consistency in your promotional materials from one event to the other. While the content and the audience may change from event to event, the philosophy underlying your promotional materials and the execution processes remain the same. No matter what type of event, you can repurpose many of your basic promotional materials to suit the audience and the occasion. Here are some way to optimize your spending on giveaways and other promotional materials:

- Create materials that are more generic in nature and can be used with only minor modifications, if any, at several events across a season or a year.
- Try to find sponsors who can subsidize your costs by including their make or name on the materials.
- Think of more economical alternatives, where possible. For example, a poster laminated on a foam board is not only cheaper but also more elegant than vinyl banners.
- Produce your basic branding elements—name tags, pens, posters—in massive quantities and keep an inventory of them.

The design components should reflect the style of your sales literature and your mass advertising. An important step is to find the right printer or producer. Your relationship with a well-chosen supplier is an important factor in the quality of the products you will get. It pays to build long-term relationships with suppliers who are customer-focused and resourceful. Long-term trust spurs a bit more quality. I generally like full-service suppliers. Once the creative groundwork—logo, signage, branding, copywriting—is complete, the services you will need from the product supplier can include design, artwork, graphics, photography, printing, production, and distribution. You may have multiple suppliers, based on your needs.

Look for companies outside your industry that make good use of giveaways and visual promotional items at their events. Fast food and soft drinks companies are generally very good at it. When you come across an idea that strikes you as a good one, make a note of it. Giveaways

Face Time

are an opportunity to use right item at the right time. The giveaways you select should have a purpose and reflect your company's ethos. You can build your inventory of giveaways and promotional materials based on your sales initiatives and business goals. Sales reps can also use these items to take along on sales calls.

Visual items you can use include banners, posters, vinyl decals, tent cards, hospitality folder with program, thank-you cards, paper or plastic cups or glasses, tablecloths, napkins, business card holders, personalized stationery, notepads, pens, name place cards, hangtags, gift cards, flyers, CDs/DVDs/USBs, binders, and agenda sheets.

Some giveaway items include coffee cups, belly hot bands for coffee cups, glasses, pens, shirts/polos, baseball caps, flower vases, candy bowls, chocolates, ties, leather items, crystal items, desk-use items, golf paraphernalia, luggage tags, tableware, DVDs/USBs, mouse pads, gift cards, lapel pins, and tie pins.

LEAD GENERATION

"Lead generation is a fairly core activity to marketing."
Chris Brogan

Nothing helps more in lead generation than recognition of a brand, and events go a long way in creating brand awareness. However, if lead generation plays an important role in your line of business, then you must integrate a specific lead generation strategy into the plan for each of your events. Events unlock opportunities; they initiate dialogue for sales people to further define and close. The CEO of Exordium Group, Ronda Farrell, estimates that by simply making use of their essential marketing benefits, you can increase lead generation from your events by 15% to 20%. Here are some questions that can help embed effective lead generation in your events:

1. How do sales people identify and profile target prospects from the attendee list? For example, by looking at demographics, attendee's qualification as target market, attendee's interests.
2. How can you use an event to foster deeper relationships with your customers and prospects? For example, if you are exhibiting at an event, the means available to engage your target audience can include using demo areas, organizing your own shows, hosting hospitality events, and landing speaking engagements.
3. How do you put in place effective initiatives and mechanisms to capture leads? For example, making notes on the back of business cards to be input into your database later, using

lead forms, magnetic strip, or barcode readers, or employing professional lead coordinators.
4. How do you measure the success of an event in lead generation? For example, turnout of decision makers, number of leads, number of shortlisted opportunities, outreach to the identified top targets, or measuring business closed.
5. What mechanisms have you put in place to determine the quality of leads? For example, leads generated can be rated as high, average, or low based on parameters such as buying authority or influence, availability of funds to make a purchase, the timeline defined for a purchase, and level of interest in the product or service.
6. How do you ensure a systematic follow-up of leads and inquiries for development and fulfilment? The value of events comes from your sales team's ability to follow up.

In order for your lead generation from events to be effective, keep the sales team involved throughout the process. Every touchpoint with an attendee is an area for potential lead capture. It also ensures that the sales force is fully prepared to engage prospects and customers before and at the event, and to follow through on leads that are generated on the back-end during the event. The key in lead capture is to know what questions to ask. The event setting is different from other face-to-face selling, in that, at an event, you are likely to have very limited time with each person. Ask only those questions that are required to determine if the person or the deal is a real prospect, and keep the questions brief and direct. Ask questions in the order of importance, lest the guest moves on or simply loses interest. If you use a questionnaire, keep it to a maximum of six to eight questions.

How to Manage Leads

Your lead management program must include an effective methodology for capturing leads, and order and revenue tracking that spans the event lifecycle.

- **Pre-event Lead Management:** Use mailers with a clear purpose. Create an events database. Prior to each event, review the attendee list with your onsite staff against a rating scale. Explain the type of lead capture mechanism you plan to use. Get complete profile information on highly rated attendees and approach them for one-on-one meetings with your executives at the event.
- **Onsite Lead Management:** Ensure a thorough onsite briefing. The success and productivity of an event will depend on the preparedness, competence, and discipline of your onsite team. Prepare and provide your team with brief contact profiles. Use a lead retrieval system onsite.
- **Post-event Lead Management:** Whether you use technology or do it manually, process the leads in your system within three business days following the event. Make sure your sales staff does call-downs on every single lead, performed quickly after the event and by the right relationship person.

6. THE TEAM

YOUR EVENT TEAM

"The achievements of an organization are the results of the combined effort of each individual."
Vince Lombardi

To plan and execute a successful event, you need to rely on a good team. Make sure the team you select has people with right skills for various roles. Lucid and effective communication is an imperative.

Assemble the Right People

The size of the team you assemble for an event depends on the size of the project as well as on the available resources. Generally, the bigger the scale of an event, the bigger the team. Don't be reluctant to ask for help. When planning your event, clearly identify to whom questions should be directed. This will reduce the time spent in resolving issues.

Your business is the very reason for your organizing the event. Make sure that different areas of your business work together to ensure that you start with the right conception and budget. Clearly communicate the deliverables to all concerned areas of the business and follow up meticulously.

Key Roles: Event Organizing

Some of the key roles involved in organizing an event are summarized below. Needless to say, an individual member can have the skills to carry out multiple roles. Conversely, very large events can require teams for various roles.

Buying Expert

Your procurement people are experts in buying at a professional level, and their experience should come in handy for event organizing. The challenge, simply put, is to get the best deals from the best suppliers. Ask your procurement expert to take a proactive approach by providing her input in the budgeting process and always providing a heads-up for any likely cost changes.

Project Manager

A project or event manager needs to be designated early on. This position ensures that the event is organized as planned, on time, and on budget. It is likely that, in addition to supervision, the project manager will share some of the direct responsibilities with his team members. The project manager's role begins with research about the aims and requirements of the event, followed by looking into options for suppliers, venue, entertainment, and so on. His next job is coordination: making sure that everything happens on time as it is supposed to and the event is executed as envisaged. This includes managing suppliers and the venue, communicating with and managing staff, and managing publicity and branding, execution, and logistics.

Production Manager

You need someone to guide the planning of your event from the production side. The production manager looks after the design, making, and form of an event, managing lighting, staging, and performances, and is involved in all technical decisions. The production manager ideally works with the creative team to evolve a theme for the event. She runs planning sessions or meetings for content development. The production manager may also suggest guest speakers, where needed.

Key Roles: Creative

Coming up with creative themes is one of the most interesting parts of putting events together. You will need one or several people to play the following roles on the more creative aspects.

Strategy Leader

The strategy leader works closely with the organizing team to outline the reasoning for the event's creative bent, and makes sure that the "unique selling point" of an event is aligned with its purpose.

Creative Leader

The creative leader infuses spirit into your event objectives with a unique identity and a resonant theme, to make sure that the event communicates your brand and key messages. This person develops an overall creative strategy, briefs the designers and production artists, and reviews the final designs and art work to make sure that they are of the highest quality.

3D Designer

This designer looks at a space and visualizes how it may be best used for your event. He helps you see what you envision by creating 3D models of the site. This role may not be needed if you use a venue that is already well set up and does not require you to bring additional props or staging.

Print Designer

The print designer works on design of the artwork and print material to be created for your event. She also ensures that your logo and brand are represented appropriately through all printed material.

Effective Team Leadership

Decision-Making

Having put a team in place, you need to ensure that the decision-making process during the build of your event ensures efficient and timely execution of the plans. Ask yourself what sign-offs are required and what decision-making process is involved. Executive approvals, for example, can have a significant knock-on effect on approval times and the ensuing execution. Clearly communicate the level of detail that senior executives want to know and which aspects they want to be involved in, so that you can run a smooth planning process.

Project Management

Once you and the team have decided on the approach to organizing an event, it is important to document the details. Draw up a complete project plan for your event, enumerating all the actions that need to be undertaken to realize the project's objectives. Some areas it includes are the following:

- **Project lead** responsible for all the approvals
- **Important objectives** to be achieved from the event
- **Responsibility,** including what each team or individual will do during the build of the event
- **Markers for accomplishing milestone steps** during the course of organizing
- **Key Performance Indicators (KPIs)** that need to be identified and measured

Effective Communication

Communication during the planning of an event is just as important as the organizing skills. The communication tools (meetings, calls, emails, texting) and the extent of their use will vary with the size and nature of your event. Even in this digital age, old-fashioned ways, like a face-to-face meeting, are still useful in event planning to elicit a quicker and more candid response.

Whether it is a meeting or a conference call, circulate your agenda in advance so that people turn up prepared. It is also an opportunity for you to make sure that all the subjects that need to be discussed are covered. And do not forget to record things in writing; written communication is essential for smooth planning of an event. Make and share status reports at regular intervals so that everyone is kept abreast of the progress and, if necessary, can voice their suggestions in time. A status report keeps everyone in the loop and provides a great paper trail.

EXTERNAL EVENT PARTNERS

"Getting good players is easy. Getting them to play together is the hard part."
Casey Stengel

In the lead-up to an event, and during its completion, you need the collaboration of a number of people outside your internal team. Having a reliable set of event partners who are happy to work with you is a big plus. If your business regularly does events, you'll want to build your own list of reliable external partners.

Top 10 External Partners

While you may not need all of them for each event, some partners you will often need are the following:

Audiovisual Provider

An audiovisual component has become an essential part of the experience at an event today. Many venues have in-house equipment and teams. However, you still need to take a look at what a venue has and consider if you need to bring in another supplier to ensure the quality you have in mind. You may be able to find a good recommendation from the people you know, as there are a lot of audiovisual suppliers with modern kits around.

Caterer

If your event involves food, be careful in your choice of caterer. Bad food can spoil the experience of an otherwise impeccable event; people do not mind if the food is not great, but they are unforgiving of bad food. Sometimes you may not have a choice, as the venue has an in-house caterer. However, you still need to be careful. Work with the caterer, do some tastings of the menu, and order changes, if required, until you get what you desire.

Remember to ask the caterers if they can serve for any dietary requirements your function may have. The more diverse your crowd—in terms of religion, culture, ethnicity, age—the bigger a range of food you will need to cater to your audience.

Props Supplier

Some creatively positioned props can add a lot of character to an event. If you provide a good brief of what you have in mind to a good prop supplier, they can come up with a wide range of suggestions to select from. They can give you useful feedback from their experience of what works, and they can add some innovations to enhance your event. Sometimes, it may be useful to speak to local theatre groups to see if they have any props that can be useful for your event.

Printer

Technology is increasingly reducing the amount of printed material required for an event. However, you still need printing for a number of items like lanyards, posters, cards, branding, and signage. Hence, a good printer, reliable but not expensive, is still an asset. Your venue should be able to recommend a printer if you do not already have a relationship with one.

Mover

You need to courier or move a number of things during the organization of any sizable event, often having to count on under-the-wire deliveries. Reliable event partners like movers, willing to go the extra mile, will be able to get you out of many a pickle.

Florist

Flowers are essential to any classy decoration, and not a place I recommend saving money. Floristry is an art and it takes a skilled florist to create beautiful and distinctive floral motifs as centerpieces as well as stage decorations. It is better to brief the florist early enough to ensure the supply in the right colors.

Performer

When your event requires a speaker or an entertainer, it may be difficult to work out who the appropriate performer will be. The person has to suit the occasion, be available on your date, and be affordable within your budget. You can either engage someone to hire a suitable performer or look for the right choice yourself. It is always advisable to add a secondary, indirect, or cumulative effect. Identify a few options before making the final choice. Sometimes a little stretch in budget can make a lot of difference in the quality of performance you are able to book. Always have a contingency plan in mind, in the event your keynote speaker or the star attraction drops out at the last moment.

Hosts

All events need hosts. These are usually your internal volunteers. However, if you do not have access to enough volunteers, you may need to hire staff. It is useful to have a relationship with a company that can find you staff on short notice. Having a partner who can provide skilled hosts for your event makes a lot of difference. From registration to the final goodbye, the hosts at your event are the people your audience interacts with most frequently, and their courtesy and professionalism make a tangible difference to your guests' experience of the event.

Party Rentals

Events require a lot of equipment and furniture, such as tents, walls, tables, chairs, barbecues, equipment, games, tableware, flatware, and linens. Not all venues have everything you need on hand. A good party rentals supplier can give you ideas about ways to add value at your event. Your party rentals supplier can provide you with more than chairs—stanchions, trestle tables, coat racks, popcorn makers, portable bars, games for adults and kids, and much more. A good relationship with party rental event partners can help you get a full range of supplies from one partner and things that you can rent at nominal value to add cachet to your event.

Pick and Pack Services

Some of your events will involve giveaways. For larger events, you may need a pick and pack service to help you put together goody bags, gifts, souvenirs, or information packs. Especially when you have several items to stuff into a tote bag for each of thousands of giveaways, you are better off outsourcing this service. Better to have suppliers who do exactly that—the time-consuming manual services that are not worth your time. Your printers or suppliers of material can often recommend reliable companies for this service.

YOUR TEAM ON THE DAY

"Teamwork makes the dream work."
Bang Gae

The quality of your team will determine the quality of your event. One of your team members will be the production manager to manage lighting, setting, staging, sound, and security. Here, let's talk about how to facilitate effective event team management on site on the day of the event.

In the Front

Front of house people from your team interact with guests and the audience. Depending on the venue, some of these people may be provided by the venue and some may be your own. These folks include the following:

Hosts

Hosts are an important part of your team. These are the first people your guests meet and, thus, they carry the image of your brand. Anyone who handles your guests on the day of the event has to be a good representative. While selecting hosts, opt for people who can sustain or enhance your image and who are trained to speak to guests. Hosts can have different roles such as welcoming people, taking registrations, showing guests around, providing expert advice, or roaming with microphones. Make sure that you organize a briefing with the hosts to explain their roles and what they should convey while talking to the guests.

Announcer

The announcer is the person who addresses your guests on the public address system, but is not the MC or the anchor. The task is to provide clear guiding information. This is a simple job that can be performed, without training, by anyone with a clear voice.

Waiters

Make sure that the waiters used at your event are properly trained and dressed. For better coordination, it is advisable to source the waiters from the event caterer.

Security

If your event requires security staff who may have to interact with your guests, make sure you have people who know how to behave with guests properly.

Backstage

Backstage roles include all those people that your guests will not know about if your event goes well. These are the people who make everything happen as you desire. The size of the backstage team involved usually depends on the size of the event. Some of these roles are the following:

Lighting and Sound

Almost all events have some elements of lighting design and sound effects. Find out if the venue has its own lighting and sound team or if you have to bring your technicians. Be sure to perform a mock execution of your sound and lighting plan before the event day.

Graphic Design

Graphic designers help design and create content for your event. Not every event requires a graphic designer; they are mostly needed for corporate or branding events. Your graphic designer should get everything ready at least two days before the event, and have an operator on site on the event day. The operator makes sure that every time you need a certain display, it is on screen.

Riggers

Riggers help you put your setting and your stage together. When you need to assemble your own stage, they help you build it. Even on an all-set venue you need riggers, because there are always things that you may want to move from one place to another.

Controller

An event controller is a must for large outdoor events, with multiple radio communication channels, where someone needs to make sure that all messages reach the right people. Smaller events do not need an event controller. Generally, the event controller is stationed in a booth with all communication channels open to liaise with concerned staff, particularly security. She records all activity throughout the event, including security incidents, number of visitors, and anything else that you'll want to know about after the event.

Show Caller

A show caller is needed at events with speakers or audiovisual content. The show caller makes sure that everybody keeps to time in accordance with an established running order. She is backstage with a clipboard and a microphone directing the crew. For a stage show, this person makes the calls for varying sound, music, lighting, and videos as required.

Helper

Your event team management should include a helper who handles all the little jobs that come up during the course of the event. Regardless of the extent of planning, there are always small things that need to be handled on the spur of the moment. The number of such people you need depends on the size of the event.

In-House Staff

If you have hired a venue, then generally they provide you with some of their own staff. Sometimes they are there to merely ensure that you adhere to the contract with the venue; other times they are available to carry out some of the functions you need performed on the day of the event. They need to be supervised by one of your people to make sure that they complete tasks as per your expectations. A technical meeting with the venue staff prior to the event is helpful in preventing any surprises.

Leading Your Team on the Day

You will enjoy leading your team on the day. Event team management is all about the hard work you have put into the preparation; it will feel worth it as you see it all coming together. Whether you have only one person with you or a large team handling the event, teamwork on the day is essential for your plans to come through.

You need to ensure clear and timely communication with your team during the live event. Here is how you go about it:

Prior Team Briefing

Get your team together prior to the event day and make sure that the roles and responsibilities are clearly defined and understood by all concerned. Set aside a few minutes for a quick meeting with the team just before the event, especially if there have been some late changes in the plan.

Security Briefing

Make sure that all security points are understood by your team so they are able to handle any emergency. These points may include the following:

- **Security procedures** in accordance with the law and the venue and your business's policies
- **Emergency and fire exits** in the venue
- The **numbers to reach out to** in the event of an accident
- Who is the **trained first aider** to contact, if required
- Any **specific security or safety issues**

Communication Channels

People must know whom to talk to for what and how the person can be reached. For bigger and well spread out events, walkie-talkies are a must. You can also set up several channels on radios for the different teams, so that each team can freely communicate among themselves, with conversation limited to those who need to participate.

Personal Identification

Personal ID is important for all involved in organizing a big event, so that people can recognize one another. The simplest way of ensuring identification is to have people wear their name badges or lanyards. If you want to get some branding mileage, you can have them all wear identical branded T-shirts.

Take Care of Your Team

The number one event team management tip? Only a happy team can deliver the performance you envisage on the day of the event. Your team may be working long hours and doing hard manual labor; the least you can do is to provide food for them. Add crew catering into your production schedule. Make sure that they work in a dry, warm, and conducive environment.

7. ORGANIZATION

ALL ABOUT TIMING

"Timing and accuracy is really what matters at the end of the day."
Carson Wentz

The timing of your event can have a huge impact on its success. Make sure that the event is held on the best date possible, and effort that may test your organizational and decision-making skills. During the preparation process, timelines are also essential to keep the project on course and determine how it all comes together on the event day.

Decide the Date

The date often links a business objective to the organization of an event. Consider the nature and objectives of the event when deciding on its timing and duration.

Milestone Occurrence: An event may relate directly to a milestone such as a product launch or the announcement of financial results.

Time of Year: Some events are best suited for a certain time of the year. For example, corporate events such as conferences and meetings are best planned during school year. Events for the general public, such as exhibitions, are better suited for weekends or school holidays. If your event is designed to seize the mood of a festive occasion, like Christmas, hold it in the build-up to that occasion.

Competitive Timing: Where warranted, carefully consider when your competitors are holding events that may compete with yours, or if other events planned at the same time may compete for the presence of the same audience. A clash of such events may be a challenge for yours.

External Factors: Public holidays, elections, major sporting events, or harsh weather can seriously impact your attendance. Research to obviate any such clash. Also study previous weather patterns during the time of the year you are planning for and do adequate contingency planning to handle any surprises.

Peak Season: Holding an event in the peak season not only limits your choices but also makes it a costlier affair. For example, holding a Christmas party in the week preceding Christmas may be considerably more expensive than holding it in the first half of December.

Financial Considerations: Apart from what you can afford to spend, also make sure that the timing is suitable for your audience and sponsors to stump up the money.

Day of Week: Once you have established during which period of the year and which month you want to hold your event, consider which day of the week best suits your objective. For example, avoid Friday for corporate events and plan events for the general public for weekends, where possible.

Time of Day: The time of day you hold your event affects both the attendance and the budget. For example, arranging for breakfast or dinner or for cocktails will entail considerable variance in cost.

Decide the Duration

An event should be long enough to fulfil its objective and short enough to retain the audience's interest. These are some factors you need to consider:

Audience: Think of the attention span of your target audience and determine if you need to include breaks in the content.

Type of Event: The type of event you are organizing affects its duration. For example, meetings last for a few hours maximum, whereas festivals or sporting events can last for days or even weeks. Generally, the longer an event, the more time consuming it is to plan.

Plan the Specifics

Once it has been set, it is very difficult to change the date of an event. Therefore, you need to program carefully with your suppliers, your audience, and the press. Here are some tools that may be helpful in time planning of your event:

Deadlines: Make a schedule that shows the milestones in the planning whose dates you can't afford to miss without impacting the delivery date. It is critical, at the beginning of the planning cycle, to establish by which date a task must be completed and who is accountable for its accomplishment. You can use any format for this schedule, such as an Excel spreadsheet or a Word document. For more complicated events, a sophisticated project management program can be acquired online. Include contingency time for all critical dates, and update this document throughout the build-up to the event. The deadline schedule will keep everyone on the team on target.

Production Schedule: A production schedule is a must for planning any sizable event. It is the bible your suppliers swear by. The production schedule should be detailed and clear enough to be used by anyone.

Rehearsals: You may need to rehearse some parts of your event, such as an awards ceremony. If that is the case, build the rehearsal time into your production schedule. Watching the rehearsal means you do not have to assume.

Load-in: This step includes assembling all of your suppliers at the venue to create your event. It tells you whether or not your planning has been successful. Organize load-in with your suppliers and the venue staff.

Setting: Consider what needs to be brought into the venue and what needs to be removed. Then think of what needs to be done after the objects that were brought in and taken out have been moved. This can, for instance, include furniture, false floor, staging, decoration, prop layout, branding, signage, power, sound, and lighting. Set-up can be time consuming and needs to be planned thoroughly.

Tear-Down: Plan and allow time for derigging and loading out after the event. Make arrangements in advance for your suppliers to start tear-down as quickly as possible. Communicate well so that everything is done in the order you have planned. Book a meeting with the venue manager to record handing the venue back.

Technical Running Order

A technical running order will keep your event day on track. It contains all of the instructions that your technical production will require during the show. For events such as an awards ceremony, where timing of the content delivery is critical, a meticulously prepared technical running order is essential for precision of delivery. It must be accurate to the minute and detailed enough to be clear to everyone for any aspect that will be in play—lighting, design, sound, music, screen, stage. A professional event manager and producer will usually turn up with their own technical running order.

Stay on Top of the Timeline

Finally, you need to ensure that someone is responsible for each element of the event's time schedule. Assign unambiguous duties. The proof of a well-prepared schedule lies in adhering to it. Do contingency planning. In the event that something affects one deliverable, account for its impact on any other timelines on the schedule.

MINDING THE DETAILS

"Success is the sum of details."
Harvey S. Firestone

Decor

While deciding on decor, look around your venue. Note the colors of carpets, floor, chairs, and walls. Also look at the range of tableware and see how well its pieces gel. Make a budget before finalizing the decor; unless you begin with a limit in mind, this item can suck up a lot of your dollars. Usually it is better to focus your budget on a particular area— for example, linens or floral arrangements—rather than peppering it in bits on several areas. When creating a look, keep in mind the feel and the mood you want to create.

Good organization goes a long way in enhancing the decor. For example, nicely presented menus, place cards, programs, name cards, and table numbers are a cost-effective way to lend beauty to your event. In Canada almost every item is available for rent; you can rent lighting, chairs, chair covers, tables, linens, cutlery, china, glassware, and any other items to exactly match the taste of your event. In terms of delivery, set-up, tear-down, and return of the rented items, determine exactly in advance what the rental company will be responsible for, what the facility staff will do, and what you will have to take care of on your own.

The centerpieces on the tables must be small enough for guests to see one another and talk over them. There is a huge range of ideas for centerpieces and you can afford to be imaginative. If you choose flowers, make sure that there is a theme to them all across the event.

Photographers

Consider how many photographers you will need and whether you need a video too. Also plan where the photographers will be placed. Always seek references and check the quality of a photographer's previous work. Brief your photographers in advance about any specific pictures to be taken or people to be specially covered. Inform the photographers when you want them to arrive and what time they can leave. Decide on the price and the turnaround time beforehand. Keep photographers' requirements, like lighting or staging, in mind. Arrange for a prior site visit for the photographers. Inform them of the dress code and make sure they are familiar with the guests you consider important.

Entertainment

Live entertainment can play an important part in enhancing an event. Choose the type of entertainment carefully. Is your event a family, community, cultural, arts, or corporate affair? Also keep in mind the guests' age profile; what will be a hit with one age group may not appeal at all to another. Use your judgement to set guidelines for the comedians, MCs, or other performers at your event.

Do some homework on the people you choose, and check their references. Prepare a detailed schedule of the happenings during the event and specify all important details in the contract. Find out about the entertainers' requirements. Do they need a dressing room? Do they have other special requirements—lighting, sound, stage, refreshments? What insurance coverage does the performance require, and who will provide it—you, the supplier, or the facility? Inform the entertainers of the dress requirements for the event.

Parting

Parting gifts are a nice way to send your guests away with a memory. These gifts do not have to be expensive, but they must be relevant and demonstrate good taste.

Remember to say thank you in the days immediately after your event. Thank your guests, thank your volunteers, and thank everyone who went out of their way to make your event a success. Make it personal and mention each by name. Try to be specific rather than making people feel that they are merely receiving a form letter as a formality.

PREPARING AND MONITORING THE BUDGET

*"Beware of little expenses. A small leak will
sink a great ship."*
Benjamin Franklin

It is imperative that you draw up a sensible budget for your event and then manage it meticulously. A budget takes some investment of time upfront, but it plays a very helpful part in your event's organization and financial administration going forward. Of course, there will be a few variances along the way, but the better researched and more realistic your original budget was, the closer it will come out to the final costs.

Be Prudent

Money is a finite resource in any business; spending decisions must be guided by keeping the end in mind. Unless you draw up a tight budget with clear objectives, events can be a black hole for financial outlay. Unrestrained expenditure is not what makes an event successful; it is how you spend the money that determines the achievement of your objectives for the event.

The amount of money, from within your means, that needs to be spent on an event depends on the value you want to get out of it. Business events are always organized for a business reason and must be able to deliver financial value. Define parameters for the return on investment (ROI) from an event and monitor the performance.

Make a Good Estimate

Events are a balancing act between the budget and the objectives. The first step is to determine how much money you can allocate to an event so that you can start planning and budgeting according to the funds available. If you are creative, you can make an event work within any realistic budget. The most memorable events I go to are where the organizers have thought carefully about how to make the most of the small things.

Key Budget Components

Once you have a rough idea of the money you can allocate to an event, you need to determine whether the amount will be enough and, if it is, how you are going to spend it. Some of the main areas of an event budget are the following:

Venue

Where an event will be hosted is often the most important part of its planning. Be aware of additional costs in addition to the venue's rent, such as extra hours that you want to use the venue for, power, house crew, and so on.

Content

Content is what happens at your event, and you need to budget for its cost. For example, if you are planning an interactive experience, its cost needs to be included. This is an area that invites creativity to keep costs low.

Entertainment

Entertainment costs vary hugely, and you need to be very sure that your ideas can be accommodated within the budget at hand. Take into account all costs—including fees, transport, and lodging—associated with the artists and the performance.

Lights, Acoustics, and Staging

The costs of a light and sound system are also an essential component of most events. These costs are influenced by your venue and what it includes. The costs of the set and staging also need to be ascertained to be included in the budget.

Furniture

You need furniture for your guests, for the ceremonies involved, and for your back-of-house needs. How much it costs varies with what the venue can provide. Sometimes you may need to source furniture from outside.

Food and Beverages

Catering forms a core element of most event budgets. You can either hire an all-in supplier or arrange in parts for ingredients, tableware, equipment, and servers. Most venues offer these services in-house.

Security

In case security measures are warranted in addition those offered by the venue, their costs need to be determined and budgeted for.

Branding

Whatever the nature of the event, your brand needs to stand out. Even at the most basic events, having your logo displayed around the event makes an impact.

Marketing

Every event needs to be marketed to make sure that the targeted audience knows about it. Marketing costs can vary widely based on the type and scale of an event.

Workforce

Whether you employ internal employees or external hires to organize an event, it does mean cost for the business. For external hires, find out if they want you to bear any other charges in addition to their daily rates. For internal employees, consider the overtime they might run up.

Miscellaneous

Take care to estimate and account for all ancillary costs associated with an event, such as insurance, permit fees, transport, and fuel.

Contingencies

Keep about 10% of your budget available for contingencies. Unforeseen expenses may well arise, especially at the last minute.

Spend Wisely

Focus on the practical things first before allocating any of your budget to nice-to-haves. In order to be able to buy well, it is important to shop around. Generally, three quotes should give you a fair sense of the prevailing range and prices for a product or service. Make sure you brief suppliers to ensure that their quotes cover all the aspects you require so that, especially in terms of services, you end up comparing like with like. Agree on the payment terms with your suppliers. Have a good grasp on your cash flow to ensure that you have sufficient funds to pay the various suppliers you use.

Mind the Contracts

Not every supplier will need a contract, but purchasing for an event can entail signing a number of contracts. You do not necessarily need legal advice, especially if you do not have an in-house lawyer, but you must read each contract you sign. For example, reading the contract you sign with the venue may provide you with some useful information for planning your event. Don't be reluctant to go back to your suppliers regarding the terms you see as troublesome or you don't understand. Keep copies of all the papers you sign. When you want to go with a quote, make sure you have it in writing. When you have to divulge confidential information to any of the suppliers, make sure that you get them to sign an NDA (Non-disclosure Agreement).

Find Sponsorships

You can find sponsors to invest money in your events in exchange for brand publicity or engagement with the audience. Be clear what you can offer to a sponsor in return for their investment and then create a sponsorship articulating your offer and the benefit to the sponsors. You can also find sponsors who provide something in return for their association with your event. Such a sponsor can offer their products at special discounts or offer special promotions to your guests. Consider trying to attract brands that you would like to be seen associated with your event. Industry bodies are also a good source of sponsorships.

Revenue Opportunities

Options for generating revenue from your event depend on the nature of the event and what the audience is likely to accept. For example, if your event has enough of a pull, you can consider selling tickets. By selling tickets, you can control numbers as well as ensure attendance, because people are more likely to turn up if they have paid even a small amount. If you allow bar sales at your event, you can negotiate a share of the sales. If your event has a strong brand, you can generate revenue by selling the items such as T-shirts or phone covers with the event's branding. Another idea is to sell a book that resonates with your audience and negotiate a fee for each book sold from the publisher.

CONTINGENCY PLANNING

"It is a bad plan that cannot be altered."
Publilius Syrus

Organizing an event invariably entails some risk as you can neither see into the future nor control everything. When planning your event, it is important to think about what may go wrong and have a plan for those contingencies that can be anticipated. Contingency planning is an important part of event planning. It is a process of asking yourself relevant "what if?" questions and being prepared if something does happen. These potential situations could be related to a number of factors, such as weather turning bad or the star attraction not turning up. Having a plan B in place is what contingency planning is about. Owing to the more expansive nature of potential problems, a contingency plan is more a conversational document than a spreadsheet, where you rely more on talking through the scenarios with your team rather than on them reading the document.

How to Plan for Contingencies

These are some steps that can help you approach contingency planning in a methodical manner:

Think of the Risks

The unsavory surprise that you reasonably fear can come to pass may either be inherent to the project, like lack of success in getting the desired audience, or external, like weather surprises. While it is not so difficult to think through the internal risks, it can be challenging to gauge the likelihood of various external factors that can go wrong, simply because the possibilities are more numerous and less under your control. Once you have identified the risks, identify which ones are probable enough to warrant contingency measures. Some of the potential risks to consider may be the following:

- Physical events like fire, flood, or bad weather
- Any illnesses or other surprises affecting your team for the event
- Political upheavals like riots, demonstrations, or strikes
- Technology failures
- Legal issues

Gauge the Impact of Those Risks

Once you have identified the risks that merit a contingency plan, group them according to the impact they would have on your event. For example, torrential rainfall or a windstorm can wreak similar consequences. Once you know the impact of an eventuality, you will be able to judge its consequences for your event. You can then plan to avoid the consequences you most want to avoid. For example, if not enough people turn up at your event, then the event looking a failure will be a more significant consequence to avoid than loss of money spent on extra food and drinks.

Make a Plan B

Once you have determined the consequences you would most like to avoid, create a plan for the situations that could unleash those consequences. This plan, of course, contains actions that you wish never to have to take. In that respect, a contingency plan is a bit like insurance. Share your contingency plan with your team and make sure that they understand the actions involved. Also make sure that every action point has a person responsible for it. Preparation for potential risks early in the process leaves you with time to communicate with your team. It also gives you plenty of time to think while choosing from alternative solutions.

An Ongoing Process

Contingency planning is a dynamic process that continues throughout the build-up to the event. As time elapses, you may be able to dismiss certain risks that are no longer relevant. On the other hand, some new risks may become palpable enough to plan for.

Insurance Protection

Make sure you have adequate insurance to provide coverage in the event of an accident. Some of the main coverages that need to be in place are employee liability insurance, professional indemnity insurance, and public liability insurance.

How to Handle Potential Scenarios

Even though each event has its own risks based on its size and nature, here are some of the more generic potential scenarios to consider:

Weather

Weather is generally one of the biggest areas of concern while organizing an event. Extreme weather conditions can not only cause you headaches in organization but also undermine your event's success. Sometimes, weather conditions in another city or country can cause delays in arrival of people or goods. However, most weather situations can be anticipated and managed. While you cannot control weather, preparation can help you control your guests' experience.

When faced with serious weather concerns, it makes sense to plan a backup site. It will not be easy to move the event to another venue, but it can sometimes be the only viable option.

Do not take the preparations at an indoor venue for granted; do your homework. For example, if you are expecting unusually hot weather, check the air-conditioning of the venue beforehand. A room full of people in hot weather takes serious cooling for it to feel comfortable. Similarly, if rain is forecast then provide space for people's umbrellas and raincoats. And make arrangements to wipe their shoes clean before moving into the main areas of your event.

Non-arrivers

To start with, have watertight contracts in place with your performers that make it very costly for them not to show up. However, there will still be times when important guests or key performers may fail to turn up with very short or no notice to you. If that happens, you have to think on your feet. Go through what else is on the program and how you can minimize the impact by reorganizing the running order or extending someone else's slot to fill in the time. If the keynote speaker does not show up, think if anyone among other speakers can be promoted to keynote speaker. Do not worry about any no-shows that the audience is unlikely to notice.

Shortage of Food

Sometimes the turnout may exceed your expectations and you risk running out of food. Stay alert as your event begins and try to ascertain from the flow of people, as they begin to arrive, if the numbers are likely to surpass your expectations. If you have that feeling, immediately discuss it with your caterers to give them time for solutions such as either getting more food or reducing the portions.

Structural Issues

To minimize surprises, make sure that a structural engineer signs off on any structure you build. In the event that a structure collapses at your event without anyone being impacted, ensure that the area is made safe and the supplier is contacted. If the collapse happens during the show, cover and seal off the area so that nobody can access it. If someone is in or on the structure when it collapses, follow the emergency plan.

Delays in Supplies

It is possible that some of your items may not arrive on time and you may have to find solutions rather than changing the format of the event. For example, if the sound is inadequate, have subtitles running on the screen. If the projector goes missing, most screens can be run from smartphones. Consult with someone imaginative about how you can make the best use of what you do have. In most cases your audience wouldn't even know that what you have resorted to is different from your original plan.

Time Overruns

Always keep some margin in the schedule, as some of the presenters will take beyond their allotted time. If that happens, make sure that the performers to follow are able to wait, as they may also have to go elsewhere. If dinner is likely to be delayed because of the overrun, inform the caterer. Also consider if it impacts any transport arrangements you may have made.

Power Outages

Most venues have standby generators. However, a power failure can be a cause for concern in an outdoor event or in an event where too many high-wattage technological contraptions are involved. If that is the case and power failure is a perceptible risk, it makes sense to have a back-up power source ready. Also devise a communication plan to implement if the venue is suddenly plunged into darkness and the public address system does not work anymore.

SAFETY

"The safety of the people shall be the highest law."
Marcus Tullius Cicero

It is your responsibility to do everything in your control to keep everyone safe at your event.

Due Diligence

You have a duty of care and need to be aware of the relevant laws to know what you are responsible for. Some of the aspects you have to take care of are as follows:

Security Requirements

The level of security needed at an event is determined by the following:

- Number of people attending
- Demographics of the guests
- Number of entrance/exit points
- Likely alcohol consumption
- VIPs in attendance

You can have various tasks performed by security guards, wardens, or volunteers. Ensure that the security guards have the appropriate license for the level of security you want them to perform. The general norm is to have one security staff per 80 people for an indoor event and one security staff per 200 people for an outdoor event. Wardens can be used for tasks that do not require a license, such as guiding guests around the site, managing crowd flows, and guarding emergency exits. If you have access to volunteers that you can rely on to represent you, they can perform the same tasks as wardens without any cost to you, beyond reimbursement of out-of-pocket expenses.

Risk Appraisal

A risk appraisal deals with recognition, assessment, and calculation of the risks involved in your event. It makes sure that all the risks are well within the tolerance levels and suggests remedial actions to further mitigate them. Some things to consider during risk appraisal are the following:

- Any elements posing danger, for example, slips and trips, weather hazards, vehicular movement, fire risk, risks for the labor on the site, crowd management, and any risk specific to the event
- In the event of a potential hazard, who will be at risk and how
- Evaluation of the severity of risk, to adopt appropriate precautions

Preventing Alcohol Abuse

It is your responsibility to ensure that your guests do not create a nuisance in the neighborhood under the influence of alcohol. You have to ensure that open bottles and drinks are not carried beyond the licensed premises. Restrict binge drinking. Encourage designated drivers and/or provide easy access to cabs. Have security staff at exits and in other appropriate places. Have sufficient light in the venue.

Keeping Children Safe

Children's safety is an important factor in any event that has children among its audience. As the host, you need to ensure that all steps to protect children are in place. Put a robust procedure in place for handling lost children. For example, exits may be closed, not allowing any children to leave until the lost child has been found. If parents want to inform the police, let them do so. If a lost child is discovered, then a staff must remain with the child until the child is reunited with their caregiver. Check the criminal record of all staff who will interact with children. If the event is especially for children, be very choosy in allowing access to adults who are not accompanied by a child.

Fire Protection

Make sure that the venue is adequately equipped for fire detection and fighting. Identify any possible sources of fire. Make sure there are enough accessible fire exits for the number of people at the event. Emergency vehicle routes should never be blocked. The staff should know where the fire-fighting equipment is located and how to use it.

People with Special Needs

If you expect disabled people in the audience, then the law requires you to make the services at your event accessible. If you hire a venue, the venue is responsible for meeting the mandatory standards. However, you still need to watch that different physical features of your venue have been made equally accessible to disabled people. If you are organizing the event on your own, make sure to organize the following in terms of physical access:

- Wheelchair ramps
- Toilets for wheelchair users
- Elevated watching area for wheelchair users

If the event involves information provided to the guests, make sure it is also available in videos and in Braille. If your content includes any shock lighting effects, inform people in advance so that people with special conditions such as epilepsy are aware. Make sure that your team is aware of all the arrangements and knows how to accommodate disabled persons in the audience.

Food

Make sure that the food service at your event meets the applicable standard legal requirements. The venue of the event must

- be hygienic and clean
- be free of bugs and rats
- offer abundant supply of potable water
- offer enough light for visibility
- offer comfortable ventilation
- contain toilets and handwashing facilities
- contain adequate drainage

Workers' Protection

Any work to be performed at a height must comply with relevant regulations, and ladders should be used only when there is no safer alternative available. Make sure that all workers wear the appropriate personal protection equipment.

Medical / First Aid

The level of onsite first aid and medical provisions the event requires depends on factors such as applicable laws and whether or not the event is an outdoor affair, the weather forecast, the duration of the event, audience profile, proximity to a medical center, and consumption of alcohol.

Administrative Paperwork

Organizing events always involves some degree of paperwork. The paperwork includes the approvals that need to be in place for you to host an event. The process of thinking through what needs to be done does help you anticipate safety aspects. For large public events, an event safety plan needs to be prepared separately. This is the document that anyone can refer to for health and safety procedures. Your event safety plan needs to be prepared well in advance and circulated to the venue, police, fire and rescue service, ambulance service, and any other regulating authority involved. A typical event safety plan contains the following information:

- A brief outline of the event
- Information about the venue—including floor plans, contacts, and directions
- A risk appraisal outlining potential risks and the measures mitigating them
- An overview of temporary structures and of any suspect infrastructure
- Information about the power supply and electrical systems
- Information about food and caterers
- Arrangements for waste disposal
- Information about the security staff handling the event
- Measures to manage crowd flows
- Information about the contractors involved
- Information about the onsite communication channels
- Availability of first aid help on the site
- Details about fire safety plans, including equipment and exits
- Information about hygiene and toilet servicing
- Requirements for internal inspection and safety validation of the site
- Facilities for people with special needs
- Incident reporting
- Details of emergency procedures and contingency plans

In addition to doing your own paperwork, be sure to obtain all necessary documents from your suppliers. Important documents to get from your contractors and keep in your records include a health and safety policy, necessary certificates for materials and structures used, and public liability insurance policy.

Crowd Management

The ability to manage crowd is essential to the success of your event, as well as to the prevention of unsavory incidents. Make sure that your venue is adequate to host the crowd you expect. Consider layout of the venue, seating arrangements, viewing areas, infrastructure, emergency exits, crowd flow patterns, and circulation areas. Use the following space guidelines for determining the crowd capacity of the venue:

- Formal dinner: 16 square feet (1.49 square meters) per person
- Seated audience: 11 square feet (1.02 square meters) per person
- Lined-up audience: 7 square feet (0.65 square meters) per person
- Standing audience: 6 square feet (0.56 square meters) per person

An important factor in crowd management is to be aware of what is going through the audience's heads. Put yourself in their shoes to anticipate their behavior. Be aware of the areas and moments that may engender a huge push from the crowd. Have staff that is adequate in numbers and skills according to the level of crowd risk associated with the event.

Incident Management

With proper preparation, damage from accidents can largely be prevented. Take the following measures if an incident occurs at your event:

- Remove the debris and clear people to make the scene safe.
- Immediately contact the appropriate emergency service.

- Clear the emergency service access to the scene.
- Start a written log on a piece of paper, noting your observations, the progress of any injured people, and any treatment provided to them by the event managers.
- Take action in accordance with the severity of the injury.
- Document the incident by answering these questions: What took place? What caused it? When did it occur? How did it occur? Where did it take place? Who was involved? What treatment was provided?

TRANSPORTATION

"Anyplace worth its salt has a parking problem."
James Castle

Begin by ascertaining where your guests are likely to come from. Have you accounted for any likely traffic jams in deciding on your event's start time? Will your guests reach the venue on their own? Where will they park and what are the parking charges?

Accessibility

To determine where it will make the most logistical sense to hold your event, consider how your guests will get to the venue. If public transport is available, how frequently and till how late? Your event's schedule and keynotes must take into account that timing. Apart from commuter traffic, another event (like a major sports event) that overlaps with yours can also impact the start time for your event.

Group Transport

If you have to spend money organizing parking space, is it more economical to arrange for group transport to bring your guests to the venue? Transporting people as a group works well for corporate employees or larger family get-togethers.

If you are arranging group travel, it will most be in coaches (buses). Coaches come in all shapes and sizes to cater to your taste, your needs, and your desired level of luxury. If it is a long journey you may want the coach to be equipped with some entertainment such as movies or a bar. For short distances, double-deckers or trolley buses can add some color. If your event lasts for the entire day, it may be more cost-effective to book two one-off transfers than to rent the coaches for the duration.

Transport for VIPs

You might consider arranging limousines for the VIPs, and to secure reserved parking for VIPs who arrive with their own limousines. If you are arranging several limousines, think of some staging. A row of lustrous limousines drawing to halt one after the other can offer an impressive sight.

Special Transport

You can also be more imaginative. For example, arrange exotic cars or convertibles for important guests. Some other unusual means of transportation to a special event include horse-drawn carriages, sleighs, canoes, gondolas, camels, and helicopters.

Parking Arrangements

Parking is an important part of the experience you want to create for your guests. Consider the number of cars you expect. For example, if it is a business event, the number of cars in relation to the number of guests may be higher than it would be for a family event. Think of means within your budget that can make the parking experience pleasant. Based on distance, weather, and what guests will be wearing, consider if you will need shuttles to transfer guests from the parking lot.

You can also arrange private valet parking to add some cachet. Make sure that the company handling the valet parking is acquainted with the site. Based on the specifics of the location, they will know how many attendants they will need for the number of cars you are expecting. Don't forget to verify that the valet parking company has satisfactory insurance coverage.

Parking for Service Providers

Consider where your suppliers and staff will park their vehicles. You don't want to clog the parking area reserved for your guests.

- Clarify with the facility whether they will arrange any street permits needed or you have to do it yourself.
- Where possible, use orange cones to clearly demarcate your designated area. They are available at nominal cost.
- If your event involves media coverage, you need to provide for the space for their trucks. Also have them set up their equipment and cables before your guests start arriving.

Help with Traffic Control

Do you need help with traffic or crowd control? If you do, then paid off-duty police, who can serve in uniform, are probably the best option. You can have some in full dress uniform or on horseback to create a halo. On the other hand, they can also be available in suits or casual dress for more discreet security services.

- Don't feel constrained by the set menus you are offered. You can work with the caterer to conjure a menu that best suits your budget. Think about what you can do differently to demonstrate ingenuity and flair. And keep in mind the cardinal rule: do not run out of food and drinks!
- Be sure to include gratuities in your food and beverages budget. Also account for taxes. If you are providing some of your drinks, determine beforehand what the corkage charges are.
- Brief all staff—caterers, in-house staff, and volunteers—in advance on how the event will unfold and what is expected of each one of them. Make sure they are motivated to make the event a success.

Style of Dining Service

- Opt for an established facility rather than trying a totally new one.
- Think about the type of food you will serve. Don't forget to include some vegetarian dishes. If you expect people to eat from napkins, make sure the portions are bite-sized and don't involve dripping sauces.
- If there are plates, make sure there are enough plates for the courses on menu. The same goes for glasses for drinks.
- When you are offering a buffet, try to have a two-sided layout with identical items on each side. This will keep two lines moving at once.
- For buffets and stand-up receptions, use plates that have a slight lip on them to keep food from spilling over.
- Tell waiters to not to scrap the plates in front of the guests while clearing; it looks unprofessional.

PARTY FARE

"There is no love sincerer than the love of food."
George Bernard Shaw

Visualize the Ambience

At the initial stage, picture the room where your event will be held. Think of the color of the walls, the floor, the curtains, the linen, and the tableware, and how you can pull them all in. Does the menu go with the color scheme? Can the room be enhanced within your budget, using lighting, chair covers, or decorations? Consider any areas of protocol to be addressed, given the relevant customs and culture. For example, is a VIP table needed?

Work Out the Details

- Start by determining your fixed costs for the venue, including any special staging or decor. Knowing these costs will determine how much you can spend on food and beverages.
- Pay attention to where the kitchen is and how the food will make its way to the guests.
- If your menu is adventurous, make sure your guests know about anything outside their usual fare. Make sure you offer choices.
- Ensure the overall food presentation looks good and offers choices that go well together.

8. FOOD AND DRINK

Know Your Venue

- Do a site inspection with the caterers to make sure they are comfortable with the layout and the kitchen facilities and equipment.
- Find out what time caterers will arrive, where the food will be prepared, and the range of tasks they will perform.
- Tell the staff to look for your go-ahead to start serving. Also ask the waiters to wait for your signal to begin tear-down. Only the host should decide when it is time for the party to end. If your guests are having a good time and want the party to continue, it is worth paying overtime charges.

Plan Your Beverages

- If the event includes a cocktail, then negotiating an open bar, where you will be billed on actual consumption, is usually to your advantage. You can also negotiate a flat rate, but then your bar will likely be limited to standard drinks.
- The rule usually is to budget for two to three drinks per person per hour. Based on that calculation and on what drinks your guests are likely to consume, you can decide what you want to include in the menu.
- While pricey drinks may not be visible, some guests, like this writer, may still ask for them. Give exact instructions to bartenders and waiters regarding special or expensive drinks. For example, how requests for additional wines are to be handled. Your bartender needs your direction.
- Have one bar and a bartender for every 40 guests.
- Consider carefully where the bars are placed to avoid overcrowding. Keep the bar area clean. Floral arrangements and decor may not be practical here.
- If you are planning a champagne toast, use champagne flutes, not champagne saucers.

BUSINESS MEALS

"Adventures are all very well in their place, but there's a lot to be said for regular meals and freedom from pain."
Neil Gaiman

Breakfast

A breakfast business meeting is always a good idea. You engage people when they are fresh and have uncluttered minds. Begin by considering the objective of the breakfast. Is it to bring people together first thing in the morning or to loosen them up for the rest of a day that they will spend together? If you are hosting your breakfast in a large hotel's restaurant, reserve an area with adequate seating for your guests.

A buffet allows people to interact and mingle. Make sure you have enough food stations to avoid crowding. Place the fringe food items, such as beverages and cereals, on separate stations. Make sure tableware and utensils are sufficient for the guests. Read the fine print when deciding on the menu prices. For example, surcharges could be applicable if the chef prepares omelets, pancakes, or other items.

If you organize a sit-down breakfast meal, avoid completely limiting the options. Offer a menu with some choices, especially if your meeting is for an extended period of time. Most people like to see variety at breakfast. In high-end locations, eating off the menu at breakfast will usually cost less than a large buffet.

These days people are becoming particularly keen on healthy meals at breakfast. Based on your budget, consider adding items like fresh fruit juices, cereals, whole grain bread, milk and soy milk, yogurt, herbal tea, and decaffeinated coffee. Finally keep in mind the season: people enjoy seasonal foods, fruits, and dry fruits.

Lunch

For a lunch during a business conference or meeting, you can either have a buffet or an outdoor BBQ. Get prior information from the guests about allergies or dietary restrictions. This will help you provide with the right mix of food in the right quantities. If you also served the guests breakfast earlier in the day, consider a different location or style at lunch.

Lunch is probably the easiest menu to choose that will please most guests. Vary the courses. If you have beef soup or carpaccio, for instance, then don't serve beef in the main course, go for fish or chicken. If the afternoon work requires sedentary periods of focus, consider a light pasta. If time is in short supply, have the tables pre-set with starters. Let waiters know how to handle requests for alcoholic drinks, especially if the meeting involves external guests or customers.

If you opt for an outdoor lunch, have a contingency plan if it should rain. Also keep in mind the sun—how sunny it will be and which areas will need shade. If it is a BBQ, don't forget to provide a couple of vegetarian options.

If the afternoon involves physical activity like a round of golf, box lunches may be the right fit.

Dinner

Dinner presents you with an abundance of choices. Your dinner can be a stand-up or a sit-down buffet, a plated dinner, casual or formal. It can also have a theme. When you host a dinner, the purpose is always more than just the meals. Define the objective for which you are bringing people together and plan your event to best fulfil that objective. For example, if you want guests to mingle and talk to one another, you are better off organizing a buffet with food stations scattered around the venue.

There are several factors to consider when deciding on the menu for a buffet dinner. Consider the temperatures the food is best served at. The food items should be able to last the duration of the buffet rather than crusting over or drying out. For example, avoid dishes using mayonnaise unless they can be kept chilled. Look for variety, so that the main course items don't mirror the appetizers.

For a sit-down dinner, decide whether you want open or pre-allotted seating. If it is pre-allotted, make sure that you arrange for the guests to easily locate their seats. For a larger dinner, tables can be numbered with nice-looking stand-up cards that suit the decor.

COCKTAILS

"A cocktail done right can really show your guests that you care."
Danny Meyer

Cocktail receptions are particularly popular in the business world; they offer a great deal of flexibility and networking for both the host and the guests. Such a reception can last from one to three hours. A lot depends on the food menu accompanying the drinks. If you are offering a dinner following cocktails, then the cocktail time should not exceed two hours. However, if you are hosting cocktails only, the reception might last up to three hours. If the timing of your cocktails encroaches on the usual dinner time, the food menu must be more extensive. In that case, also plan for more quantity of food per person and make sure that coffee is also served. Count on average guests eating about 25 hors d'oeuvres per person.

Reception Set-up

- Place a premium on the set-up for a cocktail. Choose carefully from the available options.
- A terrace with a view or a location that catches the sunset can add allure.
- A setting can be further enhanced with minimal expense, for example, by placing twinkle lights in the greenery.

- If you choose an outdoor site, be sure to visit it at night to see how it will look at the time of the day when your reception will be in progress.
- For indoor cocktails, pay attention to the layout of the room. Is it a banquet hall or a lounge that allows all guests to be in one area, or does it involve several rooms or alcoves? Too many nooks and corners may sap the vibrancy of your party.
- Food staging at a cocktail party must be aesthetic and pleasing to the eye.

Ambience

- Get a clear idea of the food and beverage arrangement before deciding on the venue. Generally, it is better to have food stations and bars, as well as passed hors d'oeuvres and drinks.
- If entertainment is planned, provide some seating for those who prefer to sit down to watch. Usually, provide seating for about 40% of the guests. The idea of cocktails is to have your guests immersed in the evening, socializing and comfortable.
- The music at cocktails should always be toned down to remain in the background. However, if there is entertainment, it should be comfortably audible.
- Also keep in mind the weather expected at the time of your reception.
- Nothing beats an outdoor area with cool breeze caressing your guests. But don't think outdoors when a hot or highly humid evening is in the cards.

Competing Events

- When several events are going on at a convention or exhibition, energy at your reception is what will hold the guests at your party. In such cases, a smaller location is a better bet than a spread out venue.

- Make the atmosphere, such as music and temperature, cozy so that the guests are in no hurry to leave.

Presentation

- When appetizers are passed, make sure there is only one food item on each tray. It gives off a sense of abundance.
- Work on the presentation of the trays and have limited number of items per tray.
- Balance your menu to cater to different tastes and to take into account your guests' dietary restrictions.
- Make sure the pieces served are small enough to be consumed without cutlery.
- Ensure that food stations are restocked quickly and the required utensils are available at each food station.
- Place the food stations and bars far enough apart to avoid congestion.
- Pay attention to clearing used glasses, plates, forks, and napkins.
- Provide high bar tables for guests to place their glasses on. Generally, account for three glasses and plates per guest.
- Have enough waiters on hand to clear efficiently.

9. GUESTS

DESIGNING THE GUEST EXPERIENCE

"Plans are nothing. Planning is everything."
Albert Einstein

At a good event, the organizer has surpassed expectations by investing extra thought into the guests' experience. That comes about because event management is more than meeting requirements of lighting, seating, food, and so on. It is about making sure that your guests have a memorable and stimulating experience, and it requires ingenuity. Whatever type of event you are hosting, consider what measures you can implement to make each guest's day a bit easier from the moment their interaction with your event begins.

Facilitate the Visitor Journey

The earliest moments of interaction after the guest's arrival are usually the following:

Guest Accreditation

Does your event require guest registration and accreditation? Accreditation can enhance a guest's feeling of being a part of your event. Make sure the accreditation desk is adequately staffed and easy to find. Consider giving VIPs a separately reserved area for accreditation and a different color of lanyard so that your staff can easily look after them throughout the event. Accreditation also makes it easier for you to control different people's access to different areas. You can also send your guests a confirmation email with a barcode so that they scan their smartphones or printed copies under the barcode reader on arrival at the event. With a unique barcode or RFID, you can offer each guest a truly personalized experience.

Cloakroom

A cloakroom is particularly important for events in winter or for corporate events where people are arriving directly from the office and have their bags with them. If the facility does not already have a cloakroom, arrange for rails and hangers and a place to securely leave briefcases. Make sure enough people are available to handle the rush at the end of the event.

Signage

Basic signage, helping your guests to find their way around, can make a huge difference to your guests' experience. You can either have staff direct people or you can provide printed signage.

Human "signage" is more expensive, but it can make a great difference in bigger events where guests need directions to different places at different times of the day.

The choice of printed signage depends on the nature of your event. For example, for an outdoor venue you will need signage that is wind-resistant and, often, waterproof. At conferences in large complexes, you will need signage with floor plans. At a festival, the signage can consist of flags that also serve to embellish the venue. Make sure that, as often as possible, your signage is reusable.

You can also opt for digital signage, which is made of screens displaying information around the place. On screens, you are also able to include messages such as tickers of tweets or the upcoming agenda.

Lost Items

Some guests are bound to misplace an item, so it makes sense to designate a place for lost items and make sure your staff are aware of the process. For larger events, lost items can also be handled by the event control office responsible for making the announcements.

Event Apps

There are some 10 billion smartphones on earth now, so almost every one of your guests will likely have one. Smartphones can be of great help in communication at your event. Event-specific apps are now common. They can be used as networking tools and to help guests plan their day. Apps are excellent for the following:

- conveying real-time information
- making the entry system easier
- allowing conversations while the room stays quiet
- providing updated floorplans that help visitors find their way around
- empowering targeted networking
- raising additional advertisement revenue by offering sponsors space in the app
- capturing data and information
- saving the hassle of massive print-outs
- being eco-friendly

Ending Well

After a successful event, make sure that your guests depart as happy as the event has made them. Alert your staff a few minutes before the event ends. Ensure that the cloakroom is sufficiently staffed. If you have giveaways, get them ready to be handed to your guests. Make sure all the logistics for leaving smoothly are in place.

Mind the Setting for Your Event

Next to the content, the most important thing for an event is the atmosphere in which that content is delivered. Once you have selected the venue, think hard how best your content can feature in it. Consider the following to make your visitors' journey around the space efficient and pleasurable:

Visualize the Space

Use computer-aided designs to develop a plan that matches your vision of the site on the event day.

Room and Seating Plans

How you decide to use a room can transform the space. Layouts can help you focus the audience's attention where you want. It may help to involve a skillful designer in how best to use a room. If you are constrained to use the same room for more than one purpose, consider altering the layout when your guests are away, so that it appears a new room when they return. The most popular seating schemes are theatre seating, banquet seating, crescent seating, and classroom seating.

Exhibition layouts, however, are entirely different; layout for a bigger exhibition can be a huge job. Be mindful of the visitor journey when planning an exhibition space. Split the space into zones, grouping similar themes or businesses. Make them identifiable through branding or by using techniques such as a different carpet color for each zone. Put the most appealing displays at the back of the exhibition to encourage guests to explore the entire site. They may discover more things of interest on their way.

Set the Stage

Depending on its nature and type, your event may require a stage. If you have speakers, find out if they like to walk around or need a lectern. Also check what microphones are needed on the stage. Think about the kind of surface the stage should have. For example, a dance performance will need a hard surface, whereas VIP seating goes better with a carpet. Keep furniture movement during the show to a minimum.

Finishing Touches

Final details—like decorations or branding—can be added to the room to accentuate the theme. Leave enough time for this stage in your planning.

Entertainment

Appropriate entertainment, from soft background music to live performances, generally enhances an event. To consider options, you need to understand the nature of the event as well as the audience.

Host

It is usually a good idea to have a host or an MC to bring together all the parts of an event's content. Skilled hosts are adept at connecting content and keeping an audience interested.

Star of the Show

The star performer is likely to be someone your audience is already familiar with—and likes. It can be a showbiz personality or a sports figure, or someone else. Your audience will generally enjoy having someone famous among them.

Music

If you go with live music, make sure the musicians have everything they need to perform—sound systems, backline and amp requirements, lighting, and so on. Carry out sound checks before the show.

Food and Drink

Food and beverages are a big part of planning an event. They are needed not just to entertain but also to help your audience network or freshen up. Think deeply what will best suit your event in terms of food and beverages.

Menu

You can design the menu to suit the type of event, style of serving, time of day, and season. You can also add a theme to your menu, to reflect the identity of your event. When it comes to food and beverages, people generally welcome attention to detail. Be heedful of your guests' dietary constraints.

Service Style

It is important to choose the right style of catering service to match the nature of your event. The style of service can vary from canapé to bowl food, buffet, plated, and street food. You can also add additional features—like cocktail bars, champagne fountains, chocolate fountains, and special effects—to add cachet.

Alcohol

If you serve alcohol at your event, then as the organizer you have a duty of care towards your guests. Also be sure to comply with all applicable laws and rules. Like with food, think carefully what is appropriate for the occasion.

Make the Memories Last

You can use various methods to record the happenings at your event.

Pictures

A picture is still worth a thousand words; taking photos, the most common method of recording memories, has been made even more ubiquitous by the smartphones. If you use a designated photographer, brief the person in detail. Great pictures from an event can also be a selling point for the event next year.

Video

While photos are a good way to preserve memories, videos are more effective when you want someone to understand the happenings at an event. Normally, a professional should make a video. However, some impromptu moments can also be recorded using smartphones.

Social Media

Be mindful that almost every memory is now shared on social media. You can harness the popularity of social media to make it a marketing platform for your event.

Streaming

Online streaming of content is a great tool for widening your event's reach. If you want to make access to online streaming more exclusive, you can implement login requirements.

MINDING YOUR GUESTS

"Our greatest asset is the guests. Treat each guest as if they are the only one!"
Anonymous

Know Your Audience

More than anything else, the success of your event depends on getting the right people to attend. If you get your target audience wrong or they fail to turn up, then all the effort invested in putting the event together will come to naught. Be clear about who your targeted audience is. In some cases, when you are looking for numbers, your invitation may be transferable. However, an effort should be made to have as many as possible of the original invitees attend the event. If you have limited number of spots and need to prioritize your guests, keep a list B handy to replace dropouts. Be mindful of the guest mix. Think how you want guests to interact at your event and then draw up the list based on your event objectives.

Prepare in Advance

Before you start looking for a venue, you must know how many people will be there and what happenings your event will include. Think about the demographics of your guests and whether they will come as couples or as singles. If corporate sponsors are purchasing a number of tables, then who is likely to be at their tables—staff, family, customers, or friends? If teenagers are also attending, do bear in mind the age requirement for consuming alcohol and the host's responsibility to verify their age when in doubt. Make sure that guest lists are ready at least a couple of months before the event, allowing you time to obtain correct addresses and to get to invitations out well ahead of time.

Invitations

Invite people suitably in advance to get a place on their calendars. If your event is scheduled in a busy season, send a save-the-date message with the date and time of the event, at least to the guests you consider most important, well in advance. Use this message to create an aura of anticipation. Also indicate by when guests can expect to receive an invitation with precise details, such as the location, dress code, or event program. If appropriate, have staff follow up with guests for RSVPs. Check with the printers in advance to allow time for printing invitations, place cards, menus, and so on. If possible, get the envelopes printed first, so that you can get them ready with addresses while waiting for the invitations. If possible, send hand-written envelopes: people like to see their names in handwriting.

Media

If you are looking for media coverage of your event, think how you will assimilate them into the proceedings. For example, will you treat them as invited guests or do you intend to hold a separate press event? Also find out their requirements for effective coverage—space for a media vehicle, a separate media room, connections for a media feed, and so on—and make arrangements to meet those needs. Provide them with prepared press kits. If live coverage is involved, then you need to ensure specific happenings at the designated times. Giving them a pleasurable experience will build good working relations with media that can be useful in future.

Children

If your guests will include children, you must keep that in mind while selecting your venue. Many hotels and venues can offer engaging supervised activities such as games, acrobats, clowns, or puppet shows. Some activities may require parents' written permission. Don't arrange any activity for which you don't have sufficient staff on hand to supervise. The party can be split into separate themes for adults and children. Make sure that your menu offers items that are palatable for young tastes. At many venues, machines for candy floss, popcorns, waffles, pretzels, and so on are easily available. They can add color and interest for minimal cost.

RECEIVING YOUR GUESTS

"A guest never forgets the host who had treated him kindly."
Homer

Pre-arrival

Plan and make sure that you are all set up before the guests start arriving. Ask each supplier how much time they will need to get ready and make sure they are allowed the time and access they require. Some set-ups are sequential and may involve several suppliers. For example, heavy equipment and the stage need to be set up before the tables are laid out and decorated. Ascertain how much time each area requires and make sure you have enough time on your hands.

Arrival Areas

Whether you are holding your event at a venue or on a charter ship, the first thing that creates an impression on your guests is the arrival area. How efficiently guests are looked after on their arrival sets the tone for the rest of your event. You want your guests to feel that they have arrived at a special occasion. Make sure that the approach to the arrival area is clean and spruced up. Remove or cover all debris and ungainly objects in sight. Pay attention to the approach to the entrance points to decide which doors your guests, suppliers, and staff will use to enter the facility. Make sure that the access to your event is convenient and clearly indicated. If you have made arrangements to transfer your guests to the venue, then how they travel to the site also sets the tone. Opt for the prettiest route, where possible.

Weather Concerns

See if the entrance is covered from the drop-off point onwards, or you may need to arrange for a canopy cover or umbrellas if rain is forecast. Also make sure that there are enough hands available to assist guests as they arrive. If it is winter, make sure that the walkways are clear of snow or sludge. Arrange with the facility or designate someone to shovel and salt the walkways. If the marble or tile floor of the approach becomes slippery when wet, you may need to lay out carpets for people to walk on. Find out if the venue has reliable insurance coverage for any injuries.

Special Displays

Special activities—like searchlights, fireworks, lighting displays, snow bursts, or a greeting band—can kindle energy and bonhomie at the moment of arrival. If you are planning any special activities to greet your guests, plan well ahead to make the necessary arrangements and obtain any permissions that may be warranted. Also visit your location to make sure that it is suitable for the activity or display you have in mind. Once they see the location, your suppliers can also make recommendations based on their past experiences.

Cloak Room

Make sure you have staff standing to direct guests to the cloak room. The closer the cloak room is to the entrance the better. For bigger events, keep movement flows in mind in order to avoid congestion. Check the capacity as well as the handling speed of the cloak room in relation to the size of the expected crowd. Does it have enough racks and hangers? Make sure you do not use wire hangers for expensive fur coats. If needed, depute more staff to ensure efficiency and speed. Depending on the nature of your event and expected weather, also keep in mind the capacity to handle umbrellas or boots. If guests are arriving directly from work, think of a secure area where they can leave their briefcases.

Guest Check-in

In many events, guests may need to register and have their names checked off the guest list. If your event involves fundraising or an auction, then credit cards of those who will bid may need to be registered. Make sure that the check-in table is staffed by professional people who are well familiar with the event. Registration tables may also be used to hand out a program and seating plan. The tables used for this purpose should be placed in a convenient area and skirted and draped to look presentable.

Other Considerations

Make sure there is a ramp on the main entrance to render it accessible to a wheelchair user.

Check if the facility provides door attendants. If not, you can hire paid off-duty policemen at reasonable cost. This will leave your staff volunteers free to mix and mingle with the guests.

Find out how the facility staff, door attendants, and ushers will be dressed. You may want them to be dressed in keeping with the occasion. If it is a corporate or themed event, you'll want them clad in themed shirts for the evening. If it is a wedding or a formal affair, you may want them to wear a formal uniform. In any case, they should be identifiable either through their dress or the badges they are wearing.

If there are other events taking place on the facility, guard the privacy of your event with properly placed and visible signs.

10. PRODUCTIVITY

HOW TO MEASURE SUCCESS

"If you can't measure it, you can't improve it."
Peter Drucker

Taking a cue from marketing organs like TV and the internet, you can learn how to measure the success of your event. You should be able to develop a measurement process to garner data in the most useful manner. You will be more focused on measuring an event's success after the event, rather than through the rush of preparation, but having a clear plan will enable you to gather the required data at every opportunity. The process starts with a set of objectives for your event. These objectives determine what to measure or follow in order to ascertain how well your event did. Also remember to align the objectives with any changes in the plan caused by external influences in the lead-up to the event.

Measurement Methods

Measurement of the impact of an event is increasingly common in the consumer industry. However, measurement can also help gauge the success of an internal event. It helps you know if the event created the desired impact and if the budget was well spent. It also gives you insight for improvement for the next event.

Forms of Evaluation

These are broadly two categories:

- **Quantitative Studies:** This method of evaluation deduces results from numerical data and its analysis. Quantitative studies require a large sampling of a wide cross-section of the subject audience. The better the quality of the sample, the more reliable the results. Generally, small sample sizes are not very accurate for quantitative research.
- **Qualitative Studies:** This method of evaluation relies on the variances in quality rather than quantity. Qualitative studies can be carried out with a smaller sample base. However, the analysis of data usually takes longer, because of its complexity. Qualitative studies usually add more dimensions to the results gathered from quantitative analysis.

Methods of Evaluation

A plethora of evaluation methods are available; you can choose the one that best suits your purpose. Some of these methods are as follows:

- **In-Person Survey:** This method is highly useful in securing immediate feedback at the event site. An in-person survey is more helpful in recording people's perceptions of the event than gathering quantified metrics.
- **Phone Survey:** A phone survey usually follows the collection of participants' phone numbers during the event. This method is most often used to conduct qualitative research.
- **Online Survey:** This method involves collecting participants' email addresses at the event and then following up with an electronic survey form. Generally, no more than 2% of the people contacted for the survey participate.
- **Digital Survey:** A digital survey is usually conducted with the help of your audience's smartphones. This approach is more

consumer-friendly, as respondents can complete a digital survey at a time that best suits them. However, it must be a short one.
- **Observation:** Observation is a low-cost method that involves watching and listening to your audience with a purpose. You may need a team of volunteers who can blend in the audience without being noticeable. In order for the results to be reliable, brief your observers thoroughly on what they need to observe and how to record it.
- **Questionnaires:** Questionnaires can be useful for gathering information from a large number of people. The method is common and people are generally comfortable with it. Based on your objectives, you can use either closed or open questions. A number of free online tools are available that enable you to set up questions, conduct surveys, and get reports.

What to Measure

What you need to measure depends on the nature and scale of your event and your objectives for it. For example, these are a few of the aspects you can measure:

Brand Experience

The brand experience is often the primary target in the consumer industry and in customer-facing events. Some measurable criteria that govern brand experience are the following:

- **Consumption:** Has the respondent purchased the brand in the past?
- **Brand Recognition:** Which of a business's brands is the respondent aware of?
- **Brand Perception:** How does the respondent rate or perceive the brand?

- **Brand Equity:** Does the respondent feel a connection to the brand?
- **Word of Mouth:** Has the respondent recommended a certain brand or received a recommendation for it?
- **Perception of the Event:** What is the respondent's opinion and understanding of the event?

Employee Experience

Employee experience is relevant to internal events. It gauges their success according to their purpose—team building, education, communication, motivation, and so on. It is usually easy to measure, as employees are a captive audience. Sometimes employee experience is determined by comparing pre-event and post-event data. Here are some things that can be measured:

- employee satisfaction with the content of the job
- employee satisfaction with the work environment
- employee happiness in working with their teams
- employee understanding of the event
- employee takeaways from the event
- employee suggestions for improving the event

Social Buzz

The result of social media campaigns is easy to measure and learn from. Some common benchmarks are the following:

- **Event Website:** Google analytics can provide you with useful information about the volume and quality of traffic on your website.
- **Twitter:** Programs like Hootsuite provide you with instant data about the number and interactivity of your followers. You can also learn how many times your brand is mentioned on Twitter and the number of people interacting with your brand.

- **Facebook:** Facebook also offers plenty of information to measure the success of any activity or campaign on that platform.

PR Lift

When building or enhancing public relations is a significant objective of your event, it should be measured too. One way is by assessing the coverage of your event in the media compared to what it would have cost to buy comparable advertisement space. You can also identify how many journalists included your key messages in their coverage.

Analyze the Results

A meaningful analysis of the results is rooted in the ability to make apt comparisons. It is hard to know whether the result is bad or good unless you have something to compare it against. Present the information in a manner that its target audience will easily understand, for example, using charts and graphs or a tabular presentation.

AFTER THE EVENT

"I did then what I knew how to do. Now that I know better, I do better."
Maya Angelou

Beyond envisaging how the event will run on the day, you also need to plan for after the event. Being prepared for the time after the event can make a difference to its success.

Learning

Every event is an opportunity to learn and to improve for the future. Ask yourself what could have been better at the event. Ask your colleagues, your suppliers, your event team, and others for the feedback on your content and your approach. They may point out areas you can improve on next time.

Leftover Provisions

There are always things left over from an event. Here are some ways to handle leftovers:

- **Stationery:** Stationery can be used for the next event. However, if it is branded for a specific issue, give it away to a school or a tutoring center.

- **Food:** Send perishable food to a suitable charity. Non-perishable items can be distributed among your staff or even be used at the next event.
- **Water Bottles:** Water bottles can be used in your office or given away to a charity.
- **Toys:** Give toys away to a local school or children's charity.
- **Gifts:** Keep your gifts for the next event.
- **Set/Stage:** Very rarely can a set be preserved for the next event, unless you are planning another event quite soon. Usually, it costs a lot more to make a stage or set that can last for more than one show, and the labor costs to tear it down and store it are significant additional expenses.

Marketing

Use the event program to speak to your guests after the event is over. Encourage continuing conversation by initiating it and providing space and opportunity. Methodically talking to your guests after the event can serve some of the following purposes:

- It goes a long way in building relationships, especially cementing a new acquaintance.
- It helps follow up on the business opportunities identified.
- It is useful for broadening the reach of your event by getting people to talk about it, especially on social networks.
- If your event will recur and you want to build a reputation, engaging your audience after the event helps build its brand and spread the word.
- If the event involved special deals or discounts, then engaging the audience after the event can help sales.
- If it had a key message, then engaging the audience after the event will remind them of the event's purpose.
- Making full use of post-event marketing opportunities can help you distinguish yourself from the competition.

If your event was mainly for customers, then ensure that all those attended are included in whatever customer relationship management (CRM) system you use.

Express Gratitude

Thank your guests and audience and also your suppliers, your team, and everyone who contributed to your event's success. Send an email or a letter, or post a simple thank-you note on people's social network sites. Where pertinent, use the thank-you note to extend conversation beyond that one event moment.

Keep the Conversation Going

The best way to stay engaged is to seek feedback from your guests and then let them know that you have paid attention to it. Where their feedback reveals passion about something, show that you have noted what they said and have taken action.

You can create a website or a social media site for your event and encourage people to post comments, photos, or videos. Now that almost everyone is armed with a smartphone, so much content is created at any event without the host having to do anything. Whether it is the content you arranged for or content other people created, it can all be valuable for keeping the conversation going and for future activity.

HOW TO MEASURE PRODUCTIVITY

"Productivity is never an accident. It is always the result of a commitment to excellence, intelligent planning, and focused effort."
Paul J. Meyer

In business, events are primarily meant to bring you and your prospects together into environments that encourage relationships and business. Unlike advertising and PR, it is difficult to develop metrics to calibrate the productivity of events. No discipline of event marketing is taught at business schools, so there are no set metrics for event measurement. However, a few companies, like ShowValue and Exhibit Surveys, have made some progress in the event measurement area. They create models for consistent cross-event measurement, working out and monitoring industry event standards.

Preferably, event-by-event measurement should be a part of your overall strategy. The process starts in lead capture and progresses to an event measurement program. Both are important indicators of an event's productivity. A badge-based system works as well in any event measurement initiative. An electronic badge is more than a security tool; it also provides you with information about who actually attended the event. You can track the attendees' presence at each session by scanning their badges.

Use Metrics

Events help selling by enabling you to qualify the leads and build relationships to get to the next steps in the sales process. Capturing all the touchpoints and the experience they generate offers you valuable planning and follow-up information. Measurement of events is about identifying what works so that you can direct your investment there. When you measure the ROI of an event, it is not only about money. In the case of an event, the return can also be measured against time and resources that could have been leveraged elsewhere. Some of the key metrics that Exhibit Surveys uses for return from events are the following:

- **ROI—Return on Investment:** ROI links the event with the sales process and evaluates long-term financial benefits.
- **ROO—Return on Objective:** ROO summarizes the fulfilment of short-term goals from the event.
- **ROE—Return on Experience:** ROE captures what you have learnt and what you got across to the target audience.
- **ROR—Return on Relationships:** ROR focuses on the reinforcement of customer loyalty.

Introducing metrics enables you to know how productive your events are and also helps you compare the productivity of different types of events. One starting point could be entwining a real-time onsite survey on customer perceptions into the event strategy. This can help you corroborate your marketing ideas, choices, and branding efforts with the live target market audience. Ask intelligent questions on actionable items—and don't ask anything that you can't implement. Sales should be included in the measurement and ROI process.

Deciding what to measure is the first challenge. The key is to define your objectives before devising the ways to measure. Normally it makes sense to pick one or two objectives of the event, based on what is important to your company, and measure them for results against the targets. For example, if a key objective is to enhance brand recognition, its fulfilment can be measured by evaluating (i) Audience quality, (ii) Quality of delivery, (iii) Media coverage, (iv) Competitive presence, and so on. Or if a key objective is direct sales generation, its achievement can be gauged by valuing (i) Number and amount of leads generated, ii) Lead conversion, and (iii) Sales opportunities.

Leverage Giveaways

Money should be the primary consideration in deciding on an event's giveaways and promotional items. Look at what it costs for the item itself, shipment to the event venue, and onsite distribution. With a considered approach, you can meaningfully reduce the cost of a giveaway program without compromising its efficiency. There are systems available that can be used to monitor and measure this component of an event strategy, for example, scanning the electronic cards to ensure one gift per attendee for the pricier items.

ShowValue uses a seven-step process to measure the productivity of events. It offers a good methodology for making sure that companies capture good and relevant information and produce a report that carries business value. Here is the process for you to use fully or partially, as warranted.

1) **Define Measurable Objectives**: Identify quantifiable objectives that back your reason to spend the money, for example, amount of sales generated, number of leads, or speaker ratings.
2) **Develop a Measurement Plan:** The plan should detail the survey methods, the target audience, and the associated timelines.
3) **Create Survey Instruments:** The choice of survey instruments is based on what the objectives are. Questions and the choices they offer must be clear, brief, and suitable for the targeted audience.

4) **Capture Data:** Effective methods to capture data must take into account traffic flow dynamics, timing, and the target audience.
5) **Tabulate Results:** Assemble the data captured and tabulate the results to know what you are looking at.
6) **Perform Business Analysis:** Analyze data to determine event value. Identify areas of success and areas that need improvement.
7) **Produce Executive Report:** Pull your findings into a highly professional executive-level report that is concise, with supporting information annexed, and leads the reader through a process of discovery.

APPENDIX: CHECKLIST FOR EVENT MATERIALS AND LOGISTICS

Item	Qty	Vendor	Date	Cost
AIR TRANSPORTATION				
Air Tickets				
Agency Fees				
Airport Fees				
Transfer Fees				
ACCOMMODATION				
Name of Hotel				
Number of Rooms				
Number of Nights				
Hotel or Resort Levy				
Mandatory Gratuities				
Fitness Club				
Commissions				

Item	Qty	Vendor	Date	Cost
GROUND TRANSFERS				
Arrival Transfers				
Departure Transfers				
Airport Porterage				
Extra Baggage Transfers				
VIP Transportation				
VENUE				
Premises				
Parking/Valet				
Security				
Decor				
Lighting				
Audiovisual				
Greeters/Crew				
Entertainment				
Staging (Set/Risers/Podium)				
Pipe Drapes				
Furniture and Equipment				
FOOD & BEVERAGES				
Reception				
Cocktail				
Breakfast				
AM Break				
Lunch				

Item	Qty	Vendor	Date	Cost
PM Break				
Dinner				
Crew Meals				
EQUIPMENT				
Electrical/Engineering				
Phones				
Internet Access				
Communication/Radios				
Computer/Printer				
Office Equipment				
TECHNOLOGY				
Multimedia Video				
Lighting and Rigging				
Audio				
Video				
Staging				
Graphics				
PRODUCTION				
Scripts				
Creative Concepts				
Photographer				

Item	Qty	Vendor	Date	Cost
LABOR HELP				
Lifts				
Local Labor				
EVENTS WITHIN EVENT				
Reception				
Main Session				
Breakout Rooms				
Evening Entertainment				
Private Meetings				
Workshops				
EXHIBITION				
Booth Design				
DISPLAY MATERIAL				
Table Tent Card				
Easels				
Standalone Signs				
Table-Top Signs				
Banners				
Posters				
Hangtags				
Stickers				
Menu Cards				

Item	Qty	Vendor	Date	Cost
Lanyards/Badges				
STATIONERY				
Agenda Sheets				
Briefing/Greeting Package				
Binders				
Envelopes				
Memo Pads				
Survey Form				
Pens				
Pencils				
Books				
FIXTURES				
Ballot Boxes/Fish Bowls				
Trash Bins				
Candy Bowls				
Tissue Boxes				
Plates and Glasses				
GIVEAWAYS				
Flyers				
Brochures				
Business Cards				
Promotional Items				

Item	Qty	Vendor	Date	Cost
GADGETS				
DVD				
Camera				
TV				